George Orwell Studies

Volume Five

No. 1

George Orwell

Publishing Office
Abramis Academic
ASK House
Northgate Avenue
Bury St. Edmunds
Suffolk
IP32 6BB
UK

Tel: +44 (0)1284 700321
Fax: +44 (0)1284 717889
Email: info@abramis.co.uk
Web: www.abramis.co.uk

Copyright
All rights reserved. No part of this publication may be reproduced in any material form (including photocopying or storing it in any medium by electronic means, and whether or not transiently or incidentally to some other use of this publication) without the written permission of the copyright owner, except in accordance with the provisions of the Copyright, Designs and Patents Act 1988, or under terms of a licence issued by the Copyright Licensing Agency Ltd, 33-34, Alfred Place, London WC1E 7DP, UK. Applications for the copyright owner's permission to reproduce part of this publication should be addressed to the Publishers.

© 2020 George Orwell Studies & Abramis Academic

ISSN 2399-1267
ISBN 978-1-84549-774-3

George Orwell Studies

Contents

Editorial
Explaining One of Orwell's Strange Prejudices — by Richard Lance Keeble — Page 3

Papers
Orwell's Scottish Ancestry and Slavery – by Darcy Moore — Page 6
Menon, Orwell and the Yeats Fascism Debate – by Jaron Murphy — Page 20
Orwell, Advertisements and the Political Economy of the Media — by Richard Lance Keeble — Page 39
Eric and Alaric: Orwell and his Shadow – by Tim Crook — Page 55

Articles
Each Herself – Fact, Fiction and Female Identity – by Ann Kronbergs — Page 67
The Hôpital Cochin and the Extraordinary Life (And Death) of Marthe Hanau – by John P. Lethbridge — Page 73
Thoughtcrime … *im Zimmer 101* – by John Rodden — Page 81
How TB Can be Traced in 'Forgotten' Spanish Civil War Letter — by Gleb Zilberstein, Svetlana Zilberstein and Pier Giorgio Righetti — Page 89

Film Review
The Hunt Reduces Orwell, Yet Again, to a Meme Theme — by Benedict Cooper — Page 92

Book reviews
Kristin Bluemel reviews *Eileen: The Making of George Orwell*, by Sylvia Topp and *The Lost Girls: Love and Literature in Wartime London*, by D. J. Taylor; Martin Tyrell on *Orwell Reconsidered*, by Stephen Ingle; and Tim Crook on *George Orwell, the Secret State and the Making of Nineteen Eighty-Four*, by Richard Lance Keeble — Page 95

Radio Review
Focusing on Five Words: Fascism, Truth, Big, Law and Love — by Norman Bissell — Page 116

Review Essay
Throwing Light on Orwell's Crucial Quarrel with Comfort — by Richard Lance Keeble — Page 120

Editors
Richard Lance Keeble — University of Lincoln
Tim Crook — Goldsmiths, University of London

Reviews Editor
Megan Faragher — Wright State University

Production Editor
Paul Anderson — University of Essex

Editorial Board
Kristin Bluemel — Monmouth University, New Jersey
Peter Marks — University of Sydney
John Newsinger — Bath Spa University
Marina Remy — Paris Sorbonne
John Rodden — University of Texas at Austin
Jean Seaton — University of Westminster
Peter Stansky — Stanford University, US
D. J. Taylor — Author, journalist, biographer of Orwell
Florian Zollmann — Newcastle University

EDITORIAL

Explaining One of Orwell's Strange Prejudices

RICHARD LANCE KEEBLE

George Orwell is often seen as a secular sage, a decent man who was not afraid to speak truth to power. Yet, he was full of contradictions, limitations – and strangely obsessive prejudices. Until quite late in life, he could see little good in Roman Catholics – bar exceptions such as Graham Greene and Evelyn Waugh – and Scotland. And the origins of these obsessions have long intrigued Orwellian biographers and commentators.

Moreover, while Orwell's deeply unpleasant anti-Semitism was all too prevalent in his early writings, this attitude rapidly changed once he learned of the horrors of the Nazi persecution of the Jews. As Michael G. Brennan comments in his excellent study of Orwell's attitudes to religion (2017): 'Indeed, from 1945, Orwell offered a strident public voice in the denunciation of anti-Semitism even though during the same period – the last five years of his life – he showed no inclination to temper or adjust his apparently pathological hatred of the Catholic hierarchy.'

Orwell's biographer Gordon Bowker locates the origins of his hatred of Roman Catholics – perhaps somewhat improbably – to his being sent at the age of five to be the lone boy in a convent school which his sister, Marjorie, was attending in Henley-on-Thames. The convent was run by French Ursulines exiled from France after religious education was banned there in 1903. According to Bowker: 'If young Eric [Blair, as he then was] was first taught by Catholic nuns as a lone boy in a school of girls, it would explain two important and enduring aspects of his complex personality – his unremitting hostility towards Roman Catholicism and an acute sense of guilt.' In 1931, Blair certainly told his Eton friend, Christopher Hollis, that he regularly read the Catholic press because 'I like to see what the enemy is up to.' His anti-clerical polemics are particularly strident in the second part of *The Road to Wigan Pier* (1937) where he lambasts the 'sentimental democratic

Richard Lance Keeble

Catholics of the type of Chesterton' who naïvely argue that the dirtiness of the poor is 'healthy'.

While fighting alongside the Republicans in the Spanish civil war in 1937, he sees the Catholic Church put its full weight behind Franco's fascist forces – and this only serves to entrench his beliefs. And he considers the hostility to the Catholics in Spain is driven largely by the economic oppression of ordinary people by landowners, industrialists and the Church. During the 1940s, in his 'As I Please' columns in *Tribune*, he accuses Catholic writers such as G. K. Chesterton and Hilaire Belloc of 'flirting with the spirit of anti-Semitism' and links Catholic and Hindu intellectuals in a community of reactionary thought. In another column, he accuses the eminent Catholics, D. B. Wyndham Lewis and J. B. Morton, of propagandising on behalf of every reactionary cause – from Mussolini, appeasement and Franco to literary censorship.

Darcy Moore's outstandingly researched and original paper in this issue provides some important background that may now help explain – at least in part – Orwell's anti-Scottish attitude. This prejudice is usually seen as a consequence of his experiences at St Cyprian's prep school and as a policeman in Burma from 1922-1927. Then, after he moved to Barnhill, on the Scottish island of Jura, in 1945, it appears to wane. Moore, however, locates Orwell's loathing of the Scots and his Blair ancestry in his knowing that they were deeply implicated in slave-owning.

According to Moore, biographers have been aware that the Blair family benefited financially from the trade in slaves and that this wealth garnered social status via an aristocratic lineage when Charles Blair (1743-1802) married Lady Mary Fane. But now, through meticulous research in the archives, Moore is able to highlight the deeper interconnections and marital alliances between the Blair, Fane, Ayscough and Michel families that emanated from the society of Jamaican planters in the eighteenth century.

Crucially, a letter from Eileen Blair to her friend Nora Myles in December 1936 provides a potted history of the Blair family suggesting that it was openly discussed. She writes: 'We are staying with the Blairs & I like it. Nothing has surprised me more, particularly since I saw the house which is very small & furnished almost entirely with paintings of ancestors. The Blairs are by origin Lowland Scottish & dull but one of them made a lot of money in slaves …'

Orwell's father, Richard Walmesley (1857-1939) was the first generation of Blairs not to profit financially from slavery since 1699 but he worked for almost 40 years organising the growing and distribution of opium for the Indian Civil Service. As Moore concludes astutely: 'It is interesting to ponder why Orwell, the literary scourge of imperialism, never wrote about his family's plantations in Jamaica but then again, nor did he explore his own father's controversial work as an opium agent.'

Richard Lance Keeble,
University of Lincoln and Liverpool Hope University

Orwell's Scottish Ancestry and Slavery

DARCY MOORE

How much did Orwell know about his Scottish ancestry? His well-known prejudice against the Scots conceivably emanated from the distaste he felt for the way wealth was accrued by his forebears. These progenitors, who owned plantations in Jamaica from 1699, had a much greater involvement with the institution of slavery than previously understood. It is probable Orwell knew more than his biographers ever uncovered about how deeply implicated his Scottish ancestors were in this immoral trade in human beings.

Keywords: Eric Arthur Blair, Orwell, Colonel John Blair, John Blair, Charles Blair, slavery, ancestry, Scotland, Darien scheme, Jamaica

George Orwell 'disliked Scots' (Bowker 2004 [2003]: xiv). This prejudice is usually explained as a consequence of Eric Blair's experiences at school and as a policeman in Burma during the 1920s (Crick and Coppard 1984: 100). But it then waned from 1945, after he moved to Barnhill, on the Scottish island of Jura (Crick 1992 [1980]: 515).

Young Eric Blair's letters to his mother from boarding school were quite cheerful (Orwell 1998 [1903-1936]: 6-19). However, in 'Such, Such Were the Joys', a posthumously published essay on childhood experiences at St Cyprian's in Eastbourne, he wrote bitterly about the school's ethos. Orwell claimed:

> The school was pervaded by a curious cult of Scotland, which brought out the fundamental contradiction in our standard of values. Flip [the headmistress] claimed Scottish ancestry, and she favoured the Scottish boys, encouraging them to wear kilts in their ancestral tartan instead of the school uniform, and even christened her youngest child by a Gaelic name. Ostensibly we were supposed to admire the Scots because they were 'grim' and 'dour' ('stern' was perhaps the key word), and irresistible on the field of battle. …The real reason for the cult of Scotland was that only very rich people could spend their summers there. And the pretended belief in Scottish superiority was a cover for

the bad conscience of the occupying English, who had pushed the Highland peasantry off their farms to make way for the deer forests, and then compensated them by turning them into servants. Flip's face always beamed with innocent snobbishness when she spoke of Scotland. Occasionally she even attempted a trace of Scottish accent. Scotland was a private paradise which a few initiates could talk about and make outsiders feel small (Orwell 1998 [1947-1948]: 377).

Orwell had nothing but criticism for the values inculcated by this educational institution but Cyril Connolly, his friend and literary editor who also attended St Cyprian's, made no mention of such a 'cult' (Connolly 2008 [1938]). Orwell had been peculiarly focused on this prejudice for some time as 'Scotchification' was a theme, evident as early as 1936, in his novel, Keep the Aspidistra Flying:

'Gordon Comstock' was a pretty bloody name, but then Gordon came of a pretty bloody family. The 'Gordon' part of it was Scotch, of course. The prevalence of such names nowadays is merely a part of the Scotchification of England that has been going on these last fifty years. 'Gordon', 'Colin', 'Malcolm', 'Donald' – these are the gifts of Scotland to the world, along with golf, whisky, porridge, and the works of Barrie and Stevenson (Orwell 1998 [1936]: 39).

Kay Ekevall, a woman friend from the mid-1930s, discovered how much he 'hated Scotsmen', witnessing Orwell cross the road rather than be introduced to the poet Edwin Muir, an Orcadian, whom he wrongheadedly believed to be a Scot:

… he just had this blind prejudice because of what he called the whisky-swilling planters in Burma that he met. So he lumped all Scotsmen together (Crick and Coppard 1984: 100).

When Orwell served with the Indian Imperial Police (1922-1927), 'Rangoon society' was 'essentially Scottish' (Curle 1923: 47). He was later to confess, in a letter written to Anthony Powell in 1936, how he liked to irritate Scotsmen:

It is so rare now-a-days to find anyone hitting back at the Scotch cult. I am glad to see you make a point of calling them 'Scotchmen', not 'Scotsmen' as they like to be called. I find this a good easy way of annoying them (Orwell 1998 [1903-1936]: 484).

Colonel Clyne Stewart (1888-1959), Superintendent of the Police Training School at Mandalay, was a Scot whom Orwell knew in Burma. One biographer described him as 'a tall, rugged Scotsman' and the epitome of the dedicated servant of the empire whom

DARCY MOORE Orwell came to dislike so much (Shelden 1991: 94). He certainly managed to annoy Stewart who, after reading Orwell's first novel, *Burmese Days* (1934), warned he would 'horse-whip' Blair if he ever met him again (Crick and Coppard 1984: 64). This intense disregard for the Scots he met during the 1920s is evident when his alter ego in the novel, John Flory, says that:

> … since his first week in Rangoon, when his burra sahib (an old Scotch gin-soaker and great breeder of racing ponies, afterwards warned off the turf for some dirty business of running the same horse under two different names) saw him take off his topi to pass a native funeral and said to him reprovingly: 'Remember laddie, always remember, we are sahiblog and they are dirt!' It sickened him, now, to have to listen to such trash (Orwell 1998 [1934]: 198).

Orwell's time in Burma is well-documented as the source of his hatred of imperialism but not so oft discussed is his suggestion the Scots had a disproportionate role in the oppression of subject races for financial benefit:

> The British Empire is simply a device for giving trade monopolies to the English – or rather to gangs of Jews and Scotchmen (Orwell 1998 [1934]: 38).

This prejudice – revealed in his letters, essays, fiction and by the testimony of friends – is not merely a result of these experiences in Burma or even his sense of mischief. There is evidence of a much more deep-seated loathing of his Blair ancestry as Orwell knew the Scots were deeply implicated in slave-owning, the most terrible of the British empire's 'monopolies' (Hall et al. 2014: 22). While researching Orwell's father's imperial career as a Sub-Deputy Opium Agent in India, two generations of ancestors, who were the origin of the Blair family's involvement with the slave-trade and previously unmentioned by Orwell scholars, came to light.

BLAIR ANCESTRY

> In the eighteenth century the Blairs had been a prosperous family with aristocratic connections … and had the income from several lucrative properties in Jamaica (Shelden 1991: 13).

The history of the Blair family in the nineteenth century is commonly told by Orwell's biographers as one of decline (Taylor 2004: 14; Bowker 2004 [2003]: 3-4). Each of the descendants of Charles Blair (1743-1802), who married the daughter of the Fane Earl of Westmorland, was less distinguished than his ancestor:

> The Blairs were pattern examples of the Victorian upper-middle class: professionally – and sentimentally – attached to

the Empire, their money mostly gone, but sustained by the thought of a fine and more prosperous past. The memory of this heritage strayed into Orwell's own inner landscapes (Taylor 2004: 14).

Orwell's father, Richard W. Blair (1857-1939), was the youngest of ten children (Stansky and Abrahams 1972: 9-10). The family fortunes, built on Jamaican sugar, rum and slaves, had diminished beyond recovery. Orwell had written, in *Keep the Aspidistra Flying* (1936), a thinly disguised portrait of his own family:

> The Comstocks belonged to the most dismal of all classes, the middle-middle class, the landless gentry. In their miserable poverty they had not even the snobbish consolation of regarding themselves as an 'old' family fallen on evil days, for they were not an 'old' family at all, merely one of those families which rose on the wave of Victorian prosperity and then sank again faster than the wave itself (Orwell 1998 [1936]: 39).

Eileen Blair, his wife, confirms this in a letter to a friend, commenting that Eric's new book shares insights into a family on 'the shivering verge of gentility' which will not be popular with the Blairs (Davison 2013 [1996]: 67).

Biographers (Stansky and Abrahams 1972; Crick 1992 [1980]; Shelden 1991; Meyers 2000; Bowker 2004 [2003] and Taylor 2004) all mention Charles Blair (1743-1802), whose wealth heralded from plantations in Jamaica, as Orwell's earliest known ancestor. However, there is a lack of certainty about the family's Scottish origins in all the biographies, and in some cases incorrect dates (Crick 1992 [1980]: 46; Taylor 2004: 14). Only Meyers and Bowker mention Scotland:

> Charles Blair, Eric's great-grandfather, was born in 1743, probably of Scottish ancestry. By way of Jamaican sugar plantations and the slave trade he became sufficiently prosperous to be an acceptable husband for Lady Mary Fane, youngest daughter of the Earl of Westmoreland, to whom he was married in 1765 (Bowker 2004 [2003]: 4).

No biographer mentions Blair ancestors prior to Orwell's great-great-grandfather, Charles Blair, but indisputable evidence shows that the family fortune was built by Charles's forebears, one who unexpectedly washed-up on Jamaican shores in 1699, two generations earlier (Lawrence-Archer 1875: 28-29; Fuertado 1896; Dobson 2011: 11; UCL 2020d; UCL 2020e; UCL 2020h). It should be noted that Stansky and Abrahams mention the Blair family may have been associated with the 'abortive Scottish Darien scheme' (Stansky and Abrahams 1972: 6). There are no supporting references or footnotes and Professor Stansky is uncertain where exactly the information was gleaned but it must have been from one of his interviews with Orwell's family, friends or acquaintances (Stansky 2019: email correspondence). Someone must have known about an ancestor who pre-dated Charles Blair (1743-1802).

Biographers have understood the Blair family benefited financially from the trade in slaves and that this wealth garnered social status via an aristocratic lineage when Charles Blair married Lady Mary Fane. However, Orwell's biographers have not recognised the deeper interconnections and marital alliances between the Blair, Fane, Ayscough and Michel families that emanated from the society of Jamaican planters in the eighteenth century (UCL 2020b; 2020c).

THE DARIEN SCHEME

> Scotland was wildly over-represented among absentee slave-owners in Britain (Hall 2014: 22).

Orwell's earliest confirmed Blair ancestor, his great-great-great-great-grandfather Colonel John Blair (1668-1728), was a survivor of the 'Darien scheme' that so disastrously failed in the late-1690s (Lawrence-Archer 1875: 28-29; Fuertado 1896; Dobson 2011: 11). The Scottish parliament had endeavoured to establish a Central American colony at the Isthmus of Darien (Panama) – a foolishly optimistic plan, disproportionate to the size of the Scottish economy – involving an attack on the Spanish at a time when England was at peace (Tombs 2014: 311). King William III ordered a boycott of the struggling colony which, as a result, soon foundered disastrously. Seven months after arriving in 1698, four hundred Scottish settlers were dead. The collapse of the colony in 1699 brought Scotland, already suffering from harvest failures, to the verge of financial collapse (ibid).

Many unmarried, disbanded army officers had flocked to the venture on reading the single-page folio sheet posted widely in coffee-houses and public squares:

> Everyone who goes on the first expedition shall receive and possess fifty acres of plantable land, and 50 foot square of ground at least in the chief city or town, and an ordinary house built thereupon by the colony at the end of 3 years (Prebble 1970: 111-112).

After the early optimism and excitement of such an audacious adventure, Blair was lucky to survive, fleeing the failed colony and settling in Jamaica in 1699, where he made the family's fortune as 'a planter' (Dobson 2011: 11).

The English had captured Jamaica from the Spanish in 1655 and by 1662 there were approximately 400 slaves on the island. The cultivation of sugarcane led directly to the number of slaves growing massively to 9,504 by 1673. The landowners acquired more slaves to do the work on the estates and by 1734 there were 86,546 slaves on the island. This increased over the next 40 years until, by 1775, some 192,787 people had been sold into slavery (Jackson 2013a).

'The Honourable Colonel John Blair' was described as 'a surgeon' and 'one of the Scotch colonists of Darien' (Lawrence-Archer 1875: 29). In 1701, this 'survivor of Darien' was elected as a member of the House of Assembly of Jamaica for St. Thomas in the East and was to 'fill many other offices of trust' in the years that followed (Jackson 2013b). He represented St Catherine, St George and Port Royal and was considered a 'major slave-owner in Jamaica' (Fuertado 1896). Blair was appointed to be the Speaker of the House of Assembly in 1715 (Cundall 1915: xvii). State papers show he was allied, or friends with other planters and politicians, including John Ayscough (British History Online 1703: Aug. 5-6) who served in the 1720s as President of the Council, Chief Justice and also Governor of Jamaica (Cundall 1915: xiv-xviii). The Ayscough clan were one of 'the most noted families in Jamaica history' (Cundall 1915: 124). Blair's son, also named John (1712-1742), was married to Mary Ayscough (UCL 2020h).

On his death in 1728, the elder Blair owned 419 slaves of whom 221 were male and 198 female; 63 were children (UCL 2020d). The total value of his estate at probate: £22,036.07 in Jamaican currency of which £10,173.5 was the estimated value of the enslaved people (Fuertado 1896). Blair was interred, along with his young second wife Elizabeth Blair (1694-1721) and other members of his family, at Saint Jago de la Vega Cathedral in Spanish Town in 1728 (Dobson 2011: 11). Inscribed on the family tomb:

> Here Lyes Interr'd the Body of ELIZABETH the late wife of JOHN BLAIR ESQ'R who departed this Life the 7th of Fber 1721, Aged TWENTY SEVEN YEARS. Likewise their Four Children JOHN, THOMAS, CHRISTIAN, and MARY. (HERE) also Lieth Interr'd ye Body of the Hon'ble JOHN BLAIR. 27th day of June 1728. Aged 60 Years (Scooter 2014).

The extent of his wealth can be understood by examining records pertaining to the East and West Prospect estates (UCL 2020b; UCL 2020c). His son, John Blair (1712-1742), by the time he was buried in the same cathedral, had amassed an even greater fortune and much more property (UCL 2020e). The 'Jamaican Quit Rent books' and probate records reveal that his son Charles (1743-1802), the first Blair mentioned in biographies of Orwell, would inherit vast tracts of land and hundreds of slaves:

... 150 acres of land in St Catherine, 930 acres in St Thomas-in-the-East, 500 acres in St Ann, 300 acres in Clarendon and 1020 acres in St Thomas-in-the-Vale, total 2900 acres ... Slave-ownership at probate: 392 of whom 211 were listed as male and 181 as female. 0 were listed as boys, girls or children. Total value of estate at probate: £20,342.91 Jamaican currency of which £12,269 currency was the value of enslaved people (UCL 2020c).

It is significant that Charles, who was born after his father's death, probably returned to Dorset in England, rather than Scotland where his grandfather was born. Charles's mother, Mary Ayscough (UCL 2020h), was connected to the Fane and Michel families, slave-owners who also had addresses in 'Wessex' (UCL 2020g). Her husband had died aged 26 and the young mother had an unborn infant to raise. There was certainly enough money to live more than comfortably back in England. Her son, Charles, was later to marry into the politically well-connected Fane family and reside at Down House, in Dorset (UCL 2020h).

The 'parish' was a Jamaican administrative unit in use from 1655. Blair plantations were extensive and located in many parishes including Saint Thomas-in-the-Vale, Clarendon, Saint-Thomas-in-the-East, Saint Ann and St Catherine. One smaller property, Blairs Pen, was used for 'livestock' (UCL 2020f). It was about 200 acres and was more likely used for cattle than slaves (ibid). Records showed that other slave-owning families – the Sinclairs, Michels and Fanes – managed the Blair family estates and finances while he was a minor and that for almost a century Orwell's ancestors were absentee landlords (UCL 2020b; 2020c; 2020f).

Jamaicans commonly have Scottish surnames at a higher rate than any other country outside of Scotland (Scottish Parliament 2015). There are more 'Campbells' per acre in Jamaica than in Scotland and one notes that:

> Colonel John Campbell from Inverary left the failed Darien experiment and came to Jamaica where he had a large family, which initiated the spread of the Campbell name all over the island. The frequency of other Scottish surnames is largely a consequence of the fact that during the period of slavery in the island, a large number of slave owners and overseers were from Scotland, *particularly from the Lowlands* (ibid, italics in the original).

The Blair family, like so many other Scots, prospered due to the incredible profitability of these Jamaican plantations that supplied rum, sugar, cattle and sheep. It is worth remembering that Orwell's father was born during 1857, into declining circumstances, due to the loss of revenue that followed the abolition of slavery.

ORWELL AND EMPIRE: THE LEGACIES OF SLAVERY

Bernard Crick, 'Blair, Eric Arthur [pseud. George Orwell] (1905-1950), political writer and essayist', ODNB [*Oxford Dictionary of National Biography*]. This entry is unusual in its explicit recognition of slave-ownership, describing Charles Blair, Orwell's great-great grandfather and the founder of the family's fortune and of its transformed social position, as 'a plantation and slave owner in Jamaica' (Hall et al. 2014: 28).

Digitisation has made invaluable historical and biographical information easily accessible via the *Legacies of British Slave-Ownership* website (UCL 2020a). When launched, it was reported in the media that the searchable database revealed Orwell's ancestors were 'one of 3,000 slave-owning families paid a total of £20m. (£1.8bn in today's prices) in compensation when slavery was abolished' (BBC 2013). Following the Acts of Parliament of 1807 and 1811 that abolished the slave trade and made it a felony, British colonies instituted registers of people who were deemed to be lawfully enslaved. Those in legal possession of enslaved people in the British colonies received compensation when slavery was officially abolished in 1834, as set out under the Abolition Act of 1833 (Hall et al. 2014: 296). In 1833, the Blair family's slaves were freed and compensation paid to trustees for the 218 enslaved people on the family's East Prospect estate (UCL 2020b). Compensation could not have been paid without records and the long lists of these people, who often have the Blair surname, make for challenging reading (Ancestry 2007).

PAPER

The authors of *Legacies of British Slave-Ownership: Colonial Slavery and the Formation of Victorian Britain* frame the discussion of this period in British and world history perceptively, positing slavery was understandably considered 'regrettable' and best 'expunged', as far as possible, from 'public memory' (Hall et al. 2014: 28). Slave-ownership permeated the British elites of the time (ibid: 294) and the authors note how rare it is in Britain for privileged families to acknowledge their ancestors' challenging imperial pasts (ibid: 28). Reassuringly, on one level, Orwell's legacy is quite different.

Bernard Crick – Orwell biographer, political theorist and democratic socialist – wrote the entry for George Orwell in the *Oxford Dictionary of National Biography*. Crick pulled no punches clearly explaining that Orwell's father was an opium agent and great-great-grandfather, a slave-owner. Hall et al. point out that the activities:

> ... of those descendants of slave-owners in the twentieth and indeed twenty-first centuries who continued to shape Britain were themselves in part legacies of slave-ownership. For example, embedded in George Orwell's description of his family

as 'lower-upper middle class' – that is, 'upper-middle class without money' – is the continuing imprint of slave-ownership: while the money derived from slavery had gone by the time of Orwell's father, the social and cultural capital acquired through slave-wealth remained, propelling the family from obscurity in Scotland and sustaining its members within the ranks of a British imperial administrative class (ibid: 3).

Crick was wrong to suggest Charles Blair was 'the founder of the family's fortune' but his analysis, that without the family's profits from slavery and the riches imperialism bought to Britain, the Blairs would have remained in 'obscurity', is sound. Eric Blair, even though his family had declined in status to 'shabby' gentility, would not have attended Eton, even as a scholarship boy without the wealth and subsequent status accrued via the revenue from those plantations in Jamaica. One could reasonably argue that not only did Orwell receive a privileged education but that his Etonian connections were critical to his later publishing success. Orwell knew he was a product of empire but politically rejected participating in any ongoing imperial legacy. He understood the paradox that all individuals with a social conscience were confronted with if they wished to live ethically, decently and honestly. Gordon Comstock, in Orwell's 1936 novel, *Keep the Aspidistra Flying*, explains this paradox:

> The mistake you make, don't you see, is in thinking one can live in a corrupt society without being corrupt oneself. After all, what do you achieve by refusing to make money? You're trying to behave as though one could stand right outside our economic system. But one can't. One's got to change the system, or one changes nothing (Orwell 1998 [1936]: 235-236).

WHAT DID ORWELL KNOW?

It is interesting to consider that a possible reason for Orwell's prejudice against his Scottish heritage, deeply embedded in his personality, was related to his dislike of the family's profits made from slavery. But how much did he know about the source of Charles Blair's wealth or his earlier ancestry? Eileen Blair, Orwell's wife, wrote a letter to her friend Norah Myles during November 1936 providing a potted version of Blair family history which confirmed they were cognisant of slave-owning ancestors:

> We are staying with the Blairs & I like it. Nothing has surprised me more, particularly since I saw the house which is very small & furnished almost entirely with paintings of ancestors. The Blairs are by origin Lowland Scottish & dull but one of them made a lot of money in slaves & his son Thomas who was inconceivably like a sheep married the daughter of the Duke of Westmorland (of whose existence I never heard) & went so grand that he

spent all the money & couldn't make more because slaves had gone out. So his son went into the army & came out of that into the church & married a girl of 15 who loathed him & had ten children of whom Eric's father, now 80, is the only survivor & they are all quite penniless but still on the shivering verge of gentility as Eric calls it in his new book which I cannot think will be popular with the family (Davison 2013 [1996]: 67).

This letter from Eileen confirms that Orwell must have known that his ancestors were 'Lowland Scottish'. Charles Blair (1743-1802) was from Dorset. There is no evidence he lived anywhere other than Jamaica (possibly) or England. Colonel John Blair (1668-1728), however, was a 'Lowland Scot', possibly from Balthyock, Perthshire, and 'the first of the family' in Jamaica (Lawrence-Archer 1875: 28). For Eileen to know that the Blairs were 'Lowland Scottish' either Eric, or his father Richard, almost certainly must have told her about ancestors that pre-dated Charles Blair.

Eric Blair was his father's only son. It seems completely reasonable to assume the family had a narrative that included their distant origins:

> Eric was keenly aware of his Blair ancestry – the procession of ghostly fore-bears, their names inscribed in the Blair family Bible inherited from his father, an oil painting of Lady Mary Blair and a set of leather-bound volumes once owned by his great-uncle, Captain Horatio Blair, to which he became sentimentally attached (Bowker 2004 [2003]: 4).

However, the Blair family bible, now in the possession of Henry Dakin (the son of Marjorie Dakin, Orwell's eldest sister) has 'a neatly-drawn family tree' only dating back to Charles Blair according to a friend of Orwell's (Fyvel 1983: 16). It would be useful to know what year the bible was published and from whom it originated.

CONCLUDING REMARKS

Kay Ekevall believed Orwell's changed attitude towards 'Scotchmen' was 'his sister's doing because she married the Scots farmer' he was 'in partnership' with on the island of Jura (Crick and Coppard 1984: 100). It is evident that Orwell's writing became much more sympathetic to the Scots after he moved to that Hebridean island. In *Tribune*, in early 1947, he wrote:

> In this country I don't think it is enough realized – I myself had no idea of it until a few years ago – that Scotland has a case against England. On economic grounds it may not be a very strong case. In the past, certainly, we have plundered Scotland shamefully, but whether it is now true that England as a whole exploits Scotland as a whole, and that Scotland

would be better off if fully autonomous, is another question. The point is that many Scottish people, often quite moderate in outlook, are beginning to think about autonomy and to feel that they are pushed into an inferior position. They have a good deal of reason. In some areas, at any rate, Scotland is almost an occupied country. You have an English or Anglicised upper-class, and a Scottish working-class which speaks with a markedly different accent, or even, part of the time, in a different language. This is a more dangerous kind of class division than any now existing in England. Given favourable circumstances it might develop in an ugly way, and the fact that there was a progressive Labour Government in London might not make much difference (Orwell 1998 [1947-1948]: 43-44).

Orwell was always willing to re-evaluate his thinking and attitudes. He believed that new ideas were possible and recognised that thinking 'an advanced civilisation need not rest on slavery' was a very new idea, indeed, and clearly not one that occurred to his Scottish ancestors who had made huge fortunes from the slave-trade (Orwell 1998 [1943-1944]: 104). It is worth noting that Orwell volunteered to voice a role in 'The Abolition of Slavery' by Venu Chitale for the BBC in August 1941:

Slave Owner: *Blair* Come here! You! Adam! You'd better jump a bit faster than that when I call you. Didn't I pay twelve hundred dollars for you? You belong to me ... me ... do you understand? Do you see this fist of mine? Hard as stone with knocking down niggers. Do you hear, me you black nigger? Now then take this whip and flog that woman ... that'll drive your silly religion out of you ...

Slave (man): *Hen*. Excuse me, mas'r, I can work night and day, but don't ask me to flog a woman ....'t aint right, mas'r ...

Slave-owner: *Blair* What, you black beast ... telling me what's right to do? You low animal! We'll have the cows answering back next. I'll show you what's right. Here, Simon, hand me that cowhide whip ... (Orwell 1998 [1940-1941]: 544).

The language was appropriately brutal, and one can only speculate about the conversation of the cast who performed the radio play. Did Orwell acknowledge the role the Blairs played in the slave-trade or other imperial economic pursuits to these peers? Orwell's father was the first generation of Blairs not to profit financially from slavery since 1699 but he had worked for almost 40 years organising the growing and distribution of opium for the British empire (Meyers 2000: 5). It is interesting to ponder why Orwell, the literary scourge of imperialism, never wrote about his family's plantations in Jamaica but then again, nor did he explore his own father's controversial work as an opium agent (Moore 2018).

The novelist Anthony Powell believed Blair wrote under the name 'Orwell', partly because he preferred a separate identity as an author, partly because he disliked the idea of family origins in Scotland (Powell 1967: 62). There has been no scholarly analysis of the impact of Orwell's Scottish progenitors on this attitude, but it appears to be a significant factor in the development of his prejudice. Eric Blair may have just been prejudiced against the Scots for the reasons usually cited by biographers and those who knew the writer. However, it does seem worth considering that the wealth Orwell's Scottish ancestors generated, from an immoral trade in human beings, contributed to this prejudice, until later in his life when he became more sympathetic to the working class Scots who were themselves victims of the imperialism he despised (Bowker 2004 [2003]: 352; Orwell 1998 [1947-1948]: 43-44).

REFERENCES

Ancestry.com (2007) *Former British Colonial Dependencies, Slave Registers, 1813-1834*, Provo, UT, USA: Ancestry.com Operations Inc. Available online at https://www.ancestry.com.au/search/collections/1129/, accessed on 20 September 2020

BBC (2013) George Orwell family among 3,000 slave-owners who received compensation, *BBC News*, 27 February. Available online at https://www.bbc.com/news/uk-21586755, accessed on 6 September 2020

Bowker, Gordon (2004 [2003]) *George Orwell*, London: Abacus

British History Online (1703) America and West Indies: August 1703, 1-5, in Calendar of State Papers Colonial, America and West Indies: Volume 21, 1702-1703, edited by Cecil Headlam (London, 1913) pp 593-609. Available online at http://www.british-history.ac.uk/cal-state-papers/colonial/america-west-indies/vol21/pp593-609, accessed on 19 September 2020

Colls, Robert (2013) *George Orwell: English Rebel*, Oxford: Oxford University Press

Connolly, Cyril (2008 [1938]) *Enemies of Promise*, Chicago: University of Chicago Press

Coppard, Audrey and Crick, Bernard (1984) *Orwell Remembered*, London: Ariel Books/BBC

Crick, Bernard (1992 [1980]) *George Orwell: A Life*, Harmondsworth, Middlesex: Penguin, second edition

Cundall, Frank (1915) *Historic Jamaica*, London: Institute of Jamaica

Curle, Richard (1923) *Into the East*, London: Macmillan

Davison, Peter (2013 [1996]) *George Orwell: A Life in Letters*, New York: Liveright

Dobson, David (2011) *Scots in Jamaica, 1655-1855*, Baltimore: Clearfield

Fuertado, W. A. (1896) *Official and Other Personages of Jamaica from 1655 to 1790 Compiled from Various Sources*. Available online at http://www.jamaicanfamilysearch.com/Members/bfeurtado01.htm, accessed on 12 September 2020

Fyvel, Tosco R. (1983) *George Orwell: A Personal Memoir*, London: Hutchinson

Hall, Catherine, Draper, Nicholas, McClelland, Keith, Donington, Katie and Lang, Rachel (2014) *Legacies of British Slave-Ownership: Colonial Slavery and the Formation of Victorian Britain*, Cambridge: Cambridge University Press, Kindle edition

Jackson, Patricia (2013a) Slaves and slavery in Jamaica, *Jamaican Family Search Genealogy Research Library*. Available online at http://www.jamaicanfamilysearch.com/Members/Barche01.htm, accessed on 12 September 2020

Jackson, Patricia (2013b) Parish of St Catherine, *Jamaican Family Search Genealogy Research Library*. Available online at http://www.jamaicanfamilysearch.com/Samples2/slavery.htm, accessed on 12 September 2020

Lawrence-Archer, James Henry (1875) *Monumental Inscriptions of the British West Indies*, London: Chatto and Windus

Meyers, Jeffrey (2000) *Orwell: Wintry Conscience of a Generation*, New York: W. W. Norton & Co.

Moore, Darcy (2018) Orwell and the appeal of opium, *George Orwell Studies*, Vol. 3, No.1 pp 83-102

Moore, Darcy (2019) Orwell's Scottish ancestry & slavery, *Darcy Moore's Blog*. Available online at http://www.darcymoore.net/2019/06/23/orwells-scottish-ancestry-slavery/, accessed on 6 September 2020

Orwell, George (1997 [1934]) *Burmese Days, The Complete Works of George Orwell*, Vol. 2, Davison, Peter (ed.) London: Secker & Warburg

Orwell, George (1997 [1936]) *Keep the Aspidistra Flying, The Complete Works of George Orwell*, Vol. 4, Davison, Peter (ed.) London: Secker & Warburg

Orwell, George (1997 [1937]) *The Road to Wigan Pier, The Complete Works of George Orwell*, Vol. 5, Davison, Peter (ed.) London: Secker & Warburg

Orwell, George (1998) *A Kind of Compulsion (1903-1936), The Complete Works of George Orwell*, Vol. 10, Davison, Peter (ed.) London: Secker & Warburg

Orwell, George (1998) *A Patriot After All (1940-1941) The Complete Works of George Orwell*, Vol. 12, Davison, Peter (ed.) London: Secker & Warburg

Orwell, George (1998) *I Have Tried to Tell the Truth: 1943-1944, The Complete Works of George Orwell*, Vol. 16, Davison, Peter (ed.) London: Secker & Warburg

Orwell, George (1998) *It Is What I Think: 1947-1948, The Complete Works of George Orwell*, Vol. 19, Davison, Peter (ed.) London: Secker & Warburg

Prebble, John (1970) *The Darien Disaster*, London: Penguin

Powell, Anthony (1967) George Orwell: A memoir, *Atlantic Monthly*, CCXX, October pp 62-68

Scooter, T. (2014) Memorial Page for John Blair: 1668-27 Jun 1728, *Find a Grave Memorial no.* 130932389, citing Spanish Town Cathedral Cemetery, Spanish Town, Saint Catherine, Jamaica. Available online at https://www.findagrave.com/memorial/130932389/john-blair, accessed on 12 September 2020

Shelden, Michael (1991) *Orwell: The Authorised Biography*, London: Heinemann

The Scottish Parliament (2015) *Scottish-Jamaican Relations: Background Info*. Available online at https://www.parliament.scot/gettinginvolved/petitions/PE01500-PE01599/PE01585_BackgroundInfo.aspx, accessed on 13 September 2020

Stansky, Peter and Abrahams, William (1972) *The Unknown Orwell*, New York: Alfred A. Knopf

Stansky, Peter (2019) Email correspondence

Taylor, D. J. (2004) *Orwell – The Life*, London: Vintage

Tombs, Robert (2014) *The English and Their History: The First Thirteen Centuries*, Penguin Books Ltd. Kindle Edition

UCL Department of History (2020a) *Legacies of British Slave-Ownership Database*, Centre for the Study of the Legacies of British Slave-Ownership, University College London. Available at https://www.ucl.ac.uk/lbs/, accessed on 6 September 2020.

UCL Department of History (2020b) East Prospect Estate [Jamaica, St Thomas-in-the-East, Surrey], *Legacies of British Slave-Ownership Database*, Centre for the Study of the Legacies of British Slave-Ownership, University College London. Available online at http://wwwdepts-live.ucl.ac.uk/lbs/estate/view/2830, accessed on 6 September 2020

UCL Department of History (2020c) West Prospect Estate [Jamaica, St Thomas-in-the-Vale], *Legacies of British Slave-Ownership Database*, Centre for the Study of the Legacies of British Slave-Ownership, University College London. Available online at http://wwwdepts-live.ucl.ac.uk/lbs/estate/view/1789, accessed on 6 September 2020

UCL Department of History (2020d) Col. John Blair, *Legacies of British Slave-Ownership Database*, Centre for the Study of the Legacies of British Slave-Ownership, University College London. Available online at http://wwwdepts-live.ucl.ac.uk/lbs/person/view/2146662173, accessed on 6 September 2020

UCL Department of History (2020e) John Blair, *Legacies of British Slave-Ownership Database*, Centre for the Study of the Legacies of British Slave-Ownership, University College London. Available online at http://wwwdepts-live.ucl.ac.uk/lbs/person/view/2146655413, accessed on 6 September 2020

UCL Department of History (2020f) Blairs Pen, *Legacies of British Slave-Ownership Database*, Centre for the Study of the Legacies of British Slave-Ownership, University College London. Available online at https://www.ucl.ac.uk/lbs/estate/view/21757, accessed on 6 September 2020

UCL Department of History (2020g) Charles William Michel, *Legacies of British Slave-Ownership Database*, Centre for the Study of the Legacies of British Slave-Ownership, University College London. Available online at https://www.ucl.ac.uk/lbs/person/view/2146636748/, accessed on 6 September 2020

UCL Department of History (2020h) Charles Blair senior, *Legacies of British Slave-Ownership Database*, Centre for the Study of the Legacies of British Slave-Ownership, University College London. Available online at https://www.ucl.ac.uk/lbs/person/view/2146636746, accessed on 6 September 2020

NOTE ON THE CONTRIBUTOR

Darcy Moore is a deputy principal at a secondary school in New South Wales. He teaches English and History and has worked as an academic in post-graduate teacher education at the University of Wollongong. His interest in Orwell began at school, thirty-seven years ago, when he was enthralled by *Animal Farm* and *Nineteen Eighty-Four*. He is currently working on a book, *Orwell in Paris*. He blogs at darcymoore.net and his Twitter handle is @Darcy1968. His Orwell collection can be accessed at darcymoore.net/orwell-collection/.

Menon, Orwell and the Yeats Fascism Debate

JARON MURPHY

This paper argues, firstly, that V. K. Narayana Menon's The Development of William Butler Yeats *(published in 1942, with the revised edition appearing in 1960) has been largely but somewhat unjustly overshadowed by Orwell's oft-cited review (*Horizon, *January 1943). Secondly, that Menon's book, therefore, merits increased recognition and appreciation, both as a sincere and insightful evaluation of Yeats as well as a key text in its own right, along with Orwell's distinctive and favourable review, in what has become a long-running debate over Yeats's alleged fascist leanings. Thirdly, and paradoxically, this paper argues that Orwell's review also merits increased recognition and appreciation for its perspicacity and power in seizing and elaborating upon Menon's alarm over Yeats's* A Vision *(dated 1925 but published in 1926, with the revised edition appearing in 1937). Lastly, it suggests that both Menon's book and Orwell's review deserve improved contextualisation, including attention to Orwell's little-known subsequent review (*Time and Tide, *April 1943) and the broader professional relationship between Orwell and Menon at the BBC.*

Keywords: fascism, journalism, Menon, Orwell, poetry, politics, Yeats, *A Vision*

In *W. B. Yeats and the Anti-Democratic Tradition* (1981), Grattan Freyer surveys the 'predominantly hostile' commentary on W. B. Yeats's politics following his death in 1939 (1981: 124). Freyer finds that Louis MacNeice was first, in *The Poetry of W. B. Yeats* (1941), to factor in Yeats's reactionary views as a significant issue for scrutiny. MacNeice wrote, for instance, of Yeats having 'had a budding fascist inside himself' (1941: 132). Freyer clarifies, however, that MacNeice 'was more puzzled than disturbed by this' (1981: 124) and that, ultimately, MacNeice considered Yeats's views 'an example of zest' (1941: 232) and Yeats 'a special case' (ibid: 231). 'The first real salvo,' Freyer asserts, 'was fired by George Orwell' in the January 1943 *Horizon* (1981: 124). According to Freyer, Orwell 'was a dogmatic believer in precisely those democratic values of progress towards a more egalitarian society that Yeats rejected, so not unnaturally' (ibid: 124) he discovered in Yeats a 'rather sinister vision of life' (Orwell 2016 [1943]: 202). Freyer claims that Orwell 'did not really like Yeats' and, in common with 'most down-to-earth Englishmen, he found Yeats's whimsy and rhetorical posturing artificial and irritating' (1981: 124-125). Nevertheless, Freyer insists, Orwell 'was too honest a critic to ignore the greatness of the poetry, and he posed squarely the question raised by the fact' (ibid: 125) that 'the best writers of our time have been reactionary in tendency' (Orwell 2016 [1943]: 207). This, Freyer adds, 'has continued to trouble posterity' (1981: 125).

Oddly, however, it is only towards the end of his account that Freyer sees fit to mention, in brackets and in passing, that Orwell was, in fact, reviewing V. K. Narayana Menon's book *The Development of William Butler Yeats* (1942 – not 1933 as dated in Freyer's text). Having quoted Orwell's conclusion that Yeats 'had the outlook of those who reach Fascism by the aristocratic route' (Orwell 2016 [1943]: 204), Freyer cites Orwell's quotation of Menon in reference to Yeats's philosophical treatise *A Vision* (1926, 1937): 'And if the greatest poet of our times is exultantly ringing in an era of Fascism, it seems a somewhat disturbing symptom' (Menon 1942: 93). 'Orwell agrees,' adds Freyer, 'and points out that Yeats's case was not an isolated one' (1981: 125). Orwell's conclusion is consistent, however, with Menon's analysis: Yeats's 'aristocratic bias … seen even in his early poetry' is highlighted almost immediately in the book and traced throughout his career by Menon (1942: 3). In addition, it is Menon who points out not only, for instance, Yeats's 'exultant acceptance of authoritarianism as the only solution' but also that Yeats was not an isolated case (ibid: 91). As Orwell also quotes from Menon: 'One did not quite realise where he was heading. And those who did, like Pound and perhaps Eliot, approved of the stand that he finally took' (1942: 92).

Oddly, too, Freyer cuts Menon out of the equation at the end of his account by selectively quoting a portion (not the whole, as it might seem to anyone not familiar with the original text) of Orwell's memorable final sentence where he affirms that 'a writer's political and religious beliefs are not excrescences to be laughed away, but something that will leave their mark even on the smallest detail of his work' (Orwell 2016 [1943]: 207). Orwell's final sentence actually begins by lauding Menon's expertise, in the context of Orwell's reflection that the 'relationship between Fascism and the literary intelligentsia badly needs investigating, and Yeats might well be the starting-point' (ibid). Orwell writes: 'He is best studied by someone like Mr Menon, who can approach a poet primarily as a poet, but who also knows that a writer's political and religious beliefs are not excrescences to be laughed away… ' (ibid). This is high praise, indeed, for Menon from Orwell but one could hardly have guessed its existence from reading Freyer's account.

JARON MURPHY

Curiously, then, the critical importance of Menon and his book, which casts Yeats and *A Vision* in an ominously fascist light and provides considerable ammunition for Orwell's 'salvo', is largely overlooked by Freyer. Moreover, Freyer's account is, in fact, a prime example of a prevailing tendency to prioritise Orwell's review at the expense of Menon's book in the longstanding scholarly debate over Yeats's alleged fascist sympathies. A recent example is Daniel Tompsett's note 132 of his Introduction, covering the debate historically, in *Unlocking the Poetry of W. B. Yeats: Heart Mysteries* (2018). Tompsett leaps from MacNeice's 'disapproval of Yeats's politics but endorsement of him as a poet' to 'George Orwell's more pointed cry of [Yeats's] Fascism', effectively airbrushing Menon completely out of the picture (2018: 26). A general neglect of Menon's book as a result of almost or entirely exclusive attention to Orwell's review has never been adequately addressed in the scholarship relating to the debate. This remains somewhat unjust to Menon primarily but also to Orwell whose review, on the whole, is very favourably disposed towards Menon and his book. Orwell quotes generously from it (having, by his own admission, never read *A Vision*) and he expressly credits Menon in various ways, not least in the final sentence as we have seen but also, for instance, maintaining Menon's centrality to the core contention of the review that 'Yeats's philosophy has some very sinister implications, as Mr Menon points out. Translated into political terms, Yeats's tendency is Fascist' (Orwell 2016 [1943]: 204).

This raises the question: what possible reasons could there be for the marginalisation of Menon in the scholarship for so many years? The simple answer, perhaps, is Orwell's fame as a journalist, essayist and novelist. As Peter Davison highlights in Volume XIV of *The Complete Works of George Orwell*, entitled *Keeping Our Little Corner Clean: 1942-1943* (2001 [1998b]), although the review was published in *Horizon* it sparked '[c]onsiderable comment and correspondence' in *The Times Literary Supplement*. This included responses from Orwell to an accusation by Charles Morgan (subsequently identified) that his review was evidence of an aberrational 'political itch' (ibid: 284) and a claim by Lord David Cecil that he was 'a word-snob' (2001 [1998]: 286). While much of the comment was negative (including from Lord Alfred Douglas, on similar grounds to Lord Cecil), it was indicative of Orwell's prominence as a journalist in literary circles by the early 1940s. Notably, the correspondence shows it was Orwell who was personally targeted. Menon is not explicitly mentioned by name in any of the relevant correspondence reproduced in Volume XIV. Orwell's heightened reputation and stature internationally since his death in 1950 have also intensified scholarly interest in his works. In the context of Orwell's high profile, it is readily understandable that the review has received far greater attention than Menon's book.

This does not, however, satisfactorily justify or explain critical mistreatment of Menon's book as peripheral or irrelevant to Orwell's review. The extent to which such disregard may relate, for instance, to the issue of race, historically and systemically, has never been considered. To scholars who have read Menon's book, it would be clear that the vantage point arising from his Indian heritage, combined with the sincerity and integrity of his approach, is what makes his evaluation of Yeats so insightful and pungent. Certainly, Menon's strangely subordinate status as a critic cannot be deemed a result of lower quality or topicality of his book in comparison to Orwell's review. Besides Orwell's praise, Menon's book received several noteworthy endorsements. On the cover of the second edition, Menon is described as 'a literary scholar of distinction' and his book as 'first-class' by E. M. Forster (Menon 1960 [1942]). Also on the cover, Menon's book is described as 'excellent' by Edwin Muir, who adds that Menon's 'intimacy of understanding' of Yeats 'is really astonishing' coming from someone 'brought up in a civilisation very remote from ours' (ibid). Menon's 'study of Yeats's poetry', Muir says, 'is probably the best that has yet appeared in English' (ibid). Moreover, Herbert J. C. Grierson discloses in his Preface that Yeats himself 'respected in Mr Menon his knowledge not only of English literature but of the poetry of his own country' (Menon 1942: xiv).

ENDURING RELEVANCE

The main purpose of this paper is, therefore, to highlight and begin to redress the imbalance, and apparent disconnect, between Orwell's review and Menon's book within the scholarship. In doing so, this paper calls for enhanced recognition and appreciation of both writers as key instigators of, and contributors to, what is still, many decades later, a continuing debate concerning Yeats and fascism. Paradoxically, while Menon's book warrants increased attention, it is also true that, for its part, Orwell's 'salvo' has never received, beyond acknowledgment of its notable initial impact, due recognition for its lasting influence on the scholarship relating to Yeats's politics. The enduring relevance of Orwell's review – and therefore, underpinning this, of Menon's book – is obscured in part in Freyer's account by seemingly contradictory yet valid statements. Despite his admission of the significance of Orwell's 'salvo' in highlighting the reactionary tendency of the best writers of the time 'which has continued to trouble posterity' (1981: 125), Freyer proceeds to suggest the review is all too brief and thus inherently limited: 'Orwell did little more than broach the problem, which is indeed a complex one' (ibid). However, Menon's more elaborate book-length study identifies the reactionary problem in the context of Yeats's oeuvre and this can be seen, in Grierson's Preface, to immediately spark debate: 'The drift of [Yeats's] thought towards authoritarianism [Menon] deplores. I cannot believe that the aristocratic bent of Yeats's mind would ever have accepted with equanimity the rule of such vulgar, brutal tyrants as Hitler and his crew' (1942: xiv). Grierson avoids the broader reactionary problem raised in part, for instance, by Menon's assertions that the infamously fascist Ezra Pound 'had a remarkable hold on Yeats' (1942: 49) and 'Yeats's elegant packet for Ezra Pound [in the revised version of *A Vision*, 1937] was very significant' in relation to Pound's conception of fascism (1942: 92). Grierson's defence of Yeats in the Preface, then, suffices to underline that Orwell's 'salvo' marks also the timely arrival of the cavalry, so to speak, in support of Menon.

While the scholarship has tended to favour Orwell's review at the expense of Menon's book, the review strongly reinforces and ultimately seeks to advance Menon's position. In this vein, Orwell deserves increased recognition and appreciation for his perspicacity and power in seizing and expanding upon Menon's alarm over Yeats's politics and *A Vision*, including in relation to renowned modernist writers like Pound and Eliot and with high regard, too, for their literary excellence. The considerable reaction to the review can be explained in part as an outcome of Orwell's command of journalism geared towards a literary readership. He duly capitalises on the obvious potential for controversy presented by Menon's stance on Yeats's politics (as Grierson's Preface indicates) and his own approval, in perceiving an interconnection between the 'literary' and the 'political', of Menon's analysis of Yeats. Utilising his gifts of keen discernment, judicious quote selection, compelling and provocative argumentation, and inimitable writing style, Orwell leverages the authority of the reviewer role to back Menon and suggest, emphatically, that Menon is best placed to keep going along the trajectory established in his book, i.e. to further analysis of the relationship between fascism and the literary intelligentsia of the time. Orwell's chief criticism, after all, is that Menon 'leaves it at that' with Yeats; and Orwell resorts to recommending, beyond the book being reviewed, that Menon pick up 'where this one leaves off' by pursuing inquiry into the political leanings of other famous writers, too (Orwell 2016 [1943]: 207).

Orwell's effort to advance Menon's position underscores, however, the limitations of both texts. The review consists merely of several pages and Orwell ultimately looks to Menon to move the investigation forward again, beyond solely Yeats to encompass the wider literary intelligentsia; whereas in the book, although Menon signals his great disquiet over Yeats's politics and the esoteric philosophy of *A Vision* in the course of examining Yeats's development, he really only turns fully in the Conclusion, of just a few pages, to a discussion of an ominously fascist Yeats. It is not surprising that Menon never produced a sequel since he explicitly confesses in the Conclusion to not wanting, and being 'a little afraid' to 'discuss the whole set of complicated relationships which exist between art and politics' (1942: 93). Nevertheless, these limitations do not negate the compressed, explosive power of the contents, and lasting influence and value, of both texts in connection with the much-disputed nature of Yeats's politics. It remains the case, today, that Menon and Orwell do, indeed, continue to trouble posterity through having foregrounded, with such acuity in the early 1940s, the complex problem that the tendency of the best writers of the time such as Yeats, Pound and Eliot was reactionary. Moreover, even as Menon's book has been unfairly overshadowed by Orwell's review, the latter has been at times quite superficially criticised or evaded by some of the foremost critics and biographers in the history of Yeats scholarship. Orwell, therefore, deserves increased recognition and appreciation, too, for his troubling of posterity by drawing upon and expertly amplifying Menon's thesis: the seminal impact, particular long-term effects and enduring relevance of his 'salvo' – greatly out of proportion to its brevity – ensure that not only he continues but, by extension, that Menon also continues, with Orwell, to haunt the scholarly debate over Yeats's alleged fascist sympathies.

FLAWED COUNTER-THESIS

The evidences of Orwell's troubling of the subsequent scholarship can be detected, for instance, in the highly controversial 'Passion and Cunning: An Essay on the Politics of W. B. Yeats' (1965) by Conor Cruise O'Brien, in which it might have been expected that Orwell and Menon would be acknowledged as forerunners and prove helpful to O'Brien in his portrayal of an 'aristocratic', 'distinctly and exultantly pro-Fascist' Yeats (1988 [1965]: 45). As Freyer says, the long essay is 'the most celebrated critique in this field' and constitutes 'a broadside attack on two fronts': firstly, 'that the poet was a political opportunist'; and secondly, that 'in his political involvements, Yeats was explicitly pro-fascist' (1981: 125-126). Oddly, however, O'Brien distances himself from Orwell, and neglects to mention Menon at all, in what could possibly be seen as a version, for criticism, of the '*Clinamen*' in Harold Bloom's famous 'anxiety of influence' theory for poetry whereby one 'swerves away' from one's precursor to whom one is indebted (Bloom 1975 [1973]: 14). This manifests as 'a corrective movement' implying the precursor 'went accurately up to a certain point, but then should have swerved, precisely in the direction' that one is moving (ibid).

O'Brien takes issue with two aspects of Orwell's review, the first being Orwell's speculation that there must be 'some kind of connection between [Yeats's] wayward, even tortured style of writing and his rather sinister vision of life' (2016 [1943]: 202). O'Brien reports that Orwell 'finds this connection, as far as he finds it at all, in Yeats's archaisms, affectations and "quaintness"' but he argues that Orwell's thesis 'does not fit very well, for the "quaintness" was at its height in the 1890s, when Yeats's vision of life was, from either an Orwellian or a Marxist point of view, at its least sinister' (1988 [1965]: 18-19). Dismissively, O'Brien adds: 'Unfortunately for Orwell's thesis, it was precisely at the moment – after the turning-point of 1903 – when Yeats's vision of life began to turn 'sinister' – aristocratic and proto-Fascist – that he began to purge his style of quaintness, and his greatest poetry was written near the end of his life when his ideas were at their most sinister' (1988 [1965]: 19).

Astonishingly, however, while O'Brien displays a sound sense of Yeats's development across his oeuvre, he does not appear to have checked (or had access to the resources to check) the publication dates of the poems Orwell quotes, apparently from memory (with some minor variations), in positing his thesis. The verifiable publication dates of these verses, in chronological order, are: 'On those that hated *The Playboy of the Western World*, 1907' in *The Irish Review*, December 1911' (Allt and Alspach 1957: 294); the First Musician's opening lyric in the play *The Only Jealousy of Emer* in 'a Cuala Press edition of January 1919' (Jeffares and Knowland 1975: 106) or '*Poetry* (Chicago) January 1919' (Allt and Alspach 1957: 784); and 'An Acre of Grass' in '*The Atlantic Monthly*, April 1938' (ibid: 575). Therefore, Orwell's examples in support of his thesis fit perfectly, in fact, into O'Brien's chronology of the emergence and zenith of a 'sinister' Yeats.

Along this trajectory, it also seems peculiar that O'Brien never relates Orwell's attention to *A Vision* (1926, 1937), which is so central to the review via Menon, to his time-frames of Yeats's ideas becoming 'most sinister'. O'Brien never expressly considers anywhere in his essay Orwell's series of bombshell statements, for instance, that: 'Yeats's philosophy [in *A Vision*] has some very sinister implications, as Mr Menon points out'; 'Translated into political terms, Yeats's tendency is Fascist. Throughout most of his life, and long before Fascism was ever heard of, he had had the outlook of those who reach Fascism by the aristocratic route'; and 'He is a great hater of democracy, of the modern world, science, machinery, the concept of progress – above all, the idea of human equality' (2016 [1943]: 204). Strangely, too, it appears generations of scholars have also not checked the dates of Yeats's poems selected by Orwell, in the context of O'Brien's dismissal; or noted the absence of Orwell's attention to *A Vision* from O'Brien's chronology of a 'sinister' Yeats. This attack on Orwell by O'Brien on the basis of a flawed counter-thesis has never been questioned and called out, it seems, within the scholarship concerning Yeats's alleged fascist leanings.

O'Brien later returns to Orwell only to dismiss him again, and permanently from the essay, albeit with an initial compliment: 'George Orwell, though critical, and up to a point percipient, about Yeats's tendencies, thought that Yeats misunderstood what an authoritarian society would be like' (1988 [1965]: 42). O'Brien is referring to Orwell's argument that 'the new authoritarian civilisation, if it arrives, will not be aristocratic, or what [Yeats] means by aristocratic' as it will 'not be ruled by noblemen with Van Dyck faces, but by anonymous millionaires, shiny-bottomed bureaucrats and murdering gangsters' (2016 [1943]: 205). O'Brien objects to what he sees as Orwell's implication of 'a degree of innocence in Yeats which cannot reasonably be postulated' (1988 [1965]: 42) and an additional implication that 'the sensitive nature of the poet would necessarily be revolted by the methods of rule of an authoritarian state' (ibid: 43). O'Brien builds a persuasive case that Yeats's 'considerable experience of practical politics' and as a public figure meant he was far from naïve and could certainly countenance and even admire rule with an iron fist (ibid). O'Brien highlights Yeats's links in Ireland to, for instance, 'strongman' politician Kevin O'Higgins, who infamously signed off seventy-seven executions (see White 1966); the leader of the fascist paramilitary movement known as the Blueshirts, Eoin O'Duffy (see McGarry 2005); and fellow members of the Senate.

Oddly, however, in singling out this small portion of Orwell's review for criticism, Orwell's argument is decontextualised by O'Brien from the bigger picture of Orwell's attention to *A Vision*. Orwell first quotes, via Menon, from *A Vision* to show that Yeats 'appears to welcome the coming age' of an aristocratic civilisation 'which is 'to be "hierarchical, masculine, harsh, surgical", and he is influenced both by Ezra Pound and by various Italian Fascist writers' (2016 [1943]: 205). Again, Orwell's attention to *A Vision* via Menon might have been expected to serve O'Brien's conception and chronology of a 'sinister' Yeats. Instead, O'Brien appears to perform a species of Bloom's '*Clinamen*', having asserted that Orwell was only 'up to a point percipient'. Yet the considerable extent to which O'Brien's treatment of Orwell remains unsatisfactory can be gauged in part from the only explicit reference to *A Vision* in his long essay, which comes, in fact, in a quotation from Yeats's letter to the novelist and playwright, Olivia Shakespear, dated 23 July 1933 about meeting Blueshirts leader O'Duffy for the first time. This reference to *A Vision* by Yeats is not commented upon by O'Brien: 'I was ready [to meet and 'talk my anti-democratic philosophy' with the Blueshirts leader], for I had just re-written for the seventh time the part of *A Vision* that deals with the future' (Wade 1954: 812). Given that a key overall argument of O'Brien's essay is that Yeats's politics 'were, in his maturity and old age, generally pro-Fascist in tendency and Fascist in practice on the single occasion when opportunity arose' (1988 [1965]: 50), i.e. Yeats's initial support for O'Duffy's Blueshirts, Orwell's review based on Menon's findings regarding *A Vision* could hardly be more pertinent.

PAPER

JARON MURPHY

O'Brien's two brief and relatively minor criticisms amount to a notably superficial and largely evasive response to Orwell's review. Yet this is more than can be said for the most celebrated defence of Yeats against the charge of fascist leanings: Elizabeth Cullingford's *Yeats, Ireland and Fascism* (1981). Just as it might have been expected that Orwell and Menon, as precursors, would be acknowledged by O'Brien and serve to aid his representation of Yeats as 'pro-fascist', so too might it have been expected that Cullingford would acknowledge and endeavour to rise to the challenge posed by Orwell and Menon to her view that Yeats was not a fascist but a (Burkean) liberal, chiefly, in politics and that Yeats's 'fantasies have been taken for his convictions' (1984 [1981]: 234). Instead, Cullingford's emphasis, as it turns out, is on seeking to refute O'Brien, primarily, on a blow-by-blow basis. Perhaps partly as a consequence of O'Brien's meagre attention to Orwell, without reference to Menon, in his essay, both Orwell and Menon are oddly consigned in Cullingford's book to the small-print listings in the Selected Bibliography rather than taken on substantively.

Cullingford is able to effectively bypass, then, Menon and Orwell as O'Brien's forerunners in presenting what Freyer deems the 'most valuable part' of her book: a 'detailed analysis of the two versions and some unpublished drafts of *A Vision*, which expound Yeats's view of history, leading, as she rightly suggests, to his exploring the possibility that fascism might be the ethos to which world history in its twentieth-century context was tending' (1981:129-130). Cullingford's combative response to O'Brien (rather than Menon and Orwell, too) also shapes what Freyer deems the 'weakest part' of her book: 'where wishful thinking leads her to gloss over Yeats's very real admiration for Mussolini's Italy as a possible model for the new state he hoped Ireland might build on the *tabula rasa* created by the British withdrawal following the 1921 Treaty' (1981: 130). It is striking, however, that Cullingford's final sentence reads almost like a repurposing of Orwell's ending to his review, where he affirms that the politics will leave its mark on the smallest details of a writer's work, to ratify her own opposite position: '[Yeats's] opinions, though not those of a social democrat, were nevertheless seldom inhumane. Since Yeats was essentially and not incidentally a political writer, and since a political substructure is apparent even in poems not overtly concerned with political themes, this fact is of the utmost importance to a student of his work' (1984 [1981]: 235). Notably, too, whereas Orwell's Yeats 'is too big a man to share the illusions of Liberalism' (2016 [1943]: 205), Cullingford's Yeats is of all political stances, 'probably closest to that of Burke's Old Whigs: an aristocratic liberalism that combined love of individual freedom with respect for the ties of the organic social group. But modern Liberals, identified as they were with *laissez-faire* capitalism, had little appeal' (1984 [1981]: 235). Cullingford's book practically spoils for, but falls short of, head-on confrontation with Orwell's review, and has also somehow escaped direct comparison, it appears, within the scholarship concerning the debate over Yeats's alleged fascist leanings.

'IRRATIONAL VIOLENCE'

However, perhaps the most surprising example of the failure to bring Menon and Orwell properly into consideration of Yeats's politics and *A Vision*, and to expressly situate their critical contributions among those of other key writers in this regard, is the second volume of R. F. Foster's acclaimed biography entitled *W.B. Yeats: A Life, Vol. II: The Arch-Poet 1915-1939* (2003). This is all the more puzzling in the context of what was already, well before 2003, a highly developed and still far from settled debate over Yeats's alleged fascist sympathies, in which O'Brien and Cullingford had long since occupied diametrically opposed positions. To his credit though, Foster does not shy away from the fascism issue in his accounts of both versions of *A Vision*. For instance, he highlights Yeats's revision of the climactic instalment, Part IV, of Book III 'Dove or Swan' for the 1937 version and speculates that a reason might be that the original text (completed by Yeats on Capri in February 1925) is 'deeply affected by contemporary European upheavals, and categorically questions the utility of democratic forms of government' (2003: 290). Significantly, too, Yeats's historical mapping of civilisation includes, in the original Part IV, what Foster describes as 'a literary reflection on what was not yet called "modernism"' (ibid: 289). The final sentence of Foster's quotation of this reflection reads: 'It is as though myth and fact, united until the exhaustion of the Renaissance, have now fallen so far apart that man understands for the first time the rigidity of fact, and calls up, by that very recognition, myth – the *Mask* – which now but gropes its way out of the mind's dark but will shortly pursue and terrify' (Yeats 2008 [1926]: 175). According to Foster, this 'last phrase betrays the political dimension behind all this' (2003: 290). Yet Orwell's foregrounding of the issue of the relation between fascism and the wider literary intelligentsia (i.e. modernists like Pound and Eliot), based on Menon's findings regarding *A Vision*, could hardly be more pertinent here.

Foster later employs the word 'sinister' (reminiscent of Orwell's repeated usage of it in reference to Yeats and *A Vision* on the basis of Menon's book, as well as O'Brien's usage of it to describe Yeats's political ideas in the poet's maturity and late life) in confirming that Yeats's immersion in the ideological currents of fascism should not be overlooked, not least in relation to *A Vision*:

> The fact that he was writing in the Italy of Mussolini, whose sinister rallying-cry about trampling on the decomposing body of the Goddess of Liberty WBY had himself quoted a year before, cannot be ignored: nor can his simultaneous plunge

JARON MURPHY

into reading seminal works of the Fascist movement. He was also discussing with Joseph Hone the formation of a distinctly undemocratic political party in Ireland. The message of *A Vision* may be aristocratic as much as determinist, but it certainly expects 'irrational violence' and totalitarian government to replace a decadent democracy. ... Democratic art had been rejected long ago by WBY; democratic politics were now condemned by association (2003:291).

As pointed out in relation to O'Brien's essay, Orwell quotes from *A Vision,* via Menon, before arguing that Yeats 'fails to see that the new authoritarian civilisation, if it arrives, will not be aristocratic, or what he means by aristocratic' (2016 [1943]: 205) – which, according to O'Brien, erroneously implies 'a degree of innocence in Yeats' politically (1988 [1965]:42). Specifically, however, Orwell quotes from 'Dove or Swan' (i.e. the same section Foster draws special attention to) where Yeats 'describes the new civilization which he hopes and believes will arrive' (2016 [1943]: 205). Yeats writes that this is to be 'an *antithetical* aristocratic civilisation in its completed form, every detail of life hierarchical, every great man's door crowded at dawn by petitioners, great wealth everywhere in a few men's hands, all dependent upon a few, up to the Emperor himself who is a God dependent on a greater God, and everywhere in Court, in the family, an inequality made law... ' (1990 [1937]: 266). These lines, with minor variations from Orwell's quotation, appear in 'Dove or Swan' in both versions of *A Vision* (in Part IV of the 1937 version and Part III of the original – see also p.157 of the original, listed in the References below). In Part XVII of Book IV 'The Great Year of the Ancients' which precedes 'Dove or Swan' in the 1937 version, Yeats explains that 'an *antithetical* dispensation obeys imminent power, is expressive, hierarchical, multiple, masculine, harsh, surgical' (1990 [1937]: 256). Such passages inform Orwell's view, via Menon, that Yeats 'appears to welcome the coming age, which is to be 'hierarchical, masculine, harsh, surgical', and he is influenced both by Ezra Pound and by various Italian Fascist writers' (2016 [1943]: 205).

It is important to note, of course, that Menon and Orwell were deeply disturbed by the revised 1937 text even though it was, as Foster explains, toned down from the original: 'Selectively quoted, and read in retrospect, "Dove or Swan" is an ominous text. That its readership was both limited and bewildered may have been to the advantage of the author's reputation, and so was his decision to drop its conclusion from the later version' (2003: 291). Foster subsequently reiterates, in his account of the revised treatise, that 'Dove or Swan' has 'some alterations, with the assertions of 1925 turned, more gingerly, into questions in 1937' (2003: 603). While neither Menon nor Orwell is likely to have been any less alarmed by 'Dove or Swan' on this account, as indicated by Orwell's view that 'the tendency of the passage [from 'Dove or Swan'] I have quoted above is obvious, and its complete throwing overboard of whatever good the past two thousand years have achieved is a disquieting symptom', the evidence of some toning down by Yeats could nevertheless be seen as potential support for Orwell's warning that 'one ought not to assume that Yeats, if he had lived longer, would necessarily have followed his friend Pound, even in sympathy' (2016 [1943]: 205).

Perhaps most striking, however, is Orwell's relevance to Foster's examination of Yeats's infamous (albeit short-lived) association with the Irish fascist movement led by Eoin O'Duffy, the so-called Blueshirts – not least Yeats's composition of 'Three Marching Songs' for the movement in late 1933 and early 1934. As we have seen in relation to O'Brien's essay, Yeats wrote a letter to Olivia Shakespear dated 23 July 1933 in which he expressed his readiness to meet the Blueshirts leader after having 'just re-written for the seventh time the part of *A Vision* that deals with the future' (Wade 1954: 812). Orwell refers to Yeats's association with the Blueshirts in his response to Charles Morgan's accusation in *The Times Literary Supplement* that 'now and then, the political itch overcomes' Orwell in the review (Davison 2001 [1998]: 284). Orwell writes: 'But apart from these quotations [from *A Vision*], the facts are notorious. Did not Yeats write a "marching song" for O'Duffy's Blueshirts?' (2001 [1998]: 285-286). The third song as it was first published, for instance, clearly has parallels with 'Dove or Swan' in its depiction of hierarchy and inequality, although the connection between these two texts is not explicitly shown by Orwell and Foster:

'Soldiers take pride in saluting their Captain,

The devotee proffers a knee to his Lord,

Some take delight in adorning a woman.

What's equality – Muck in the yard:

Historic Nations grow

From above to below' (Foster 2003: 478).

As we have seen, O'Brien takes issue with Orwell's speculation that 'there must be some kind of connection between [Yeats's] wayward, even tortured style of writing and his rather sinister vision of life' (2016 [1943]: 202). Notably, Foster argues that Yeats's interest in fascism was 'partly a question of cultivating a furious style *pour épater* the Irish bourgeoisie' (2003: 482); and Foster's ending, which readily brings Orwell's speculation on Yeats's style to mind, might be purposely allusive: 'To an extent perhaps unrecognized, WBY's affinity with Fascism (not National Socialism) was a matter of rhetorical style; and the achievement of style, as he himself had decreed long before, was closely connected to shock tactics'

(2003: 483). As W. J. McCormack observes in *Blood Kindred: W. B. Yeats – The Life, The Death, The Politics* (2005), Foster's position is not, of course, the same as Orwell's. McCormack comments disapprovingly of Foster that the 'difference between Orwell and Foster is more real than apparent'. He adds: 'The former holds that the poet's politics could (ideally at least) be understood through an analysis of his style. The latter suggests that the style (understood as a superficial end-in-itself) is all that the politics amounts to' (ibid: 431).

UNANSWERED CHALLENGE

As this stinging criticism of Foster indicates, McCormack's book is noteworthy for its recognition of the enduring relevance of Orwell's review to scholarship concerning Yeats's politics. McCormack's book is also significant, however, for its explicit acknowledgement of the continuing importance of Menon's book, too. Although McCormack deals with Menon's book to a lesser degree, his positive representation of both Menon's book and Orwell's review, in conjunction, marks a departure from the prevailing scholarship. McCormack turns approvingly at times to both writers (whereas he takes issue with others, including Foster and Cullingford) in the course of reinvigorating the profile of a 'sinister' Yeats who, McCormack concludes, 'was fascist on (for me) too many occasions' (2005: 433). Unusually, for instance, McCormack refers to Menon and Orwell on equal footing and in chronological order (albeit incorrectly stating that publication of Menon's book occurred in 1943, when it was in fact 1942, and reducing Yeats's forenames to initials in the title): 'Publishing in 1943, the biographer-scholar V. K. N. Menon noted the sinister side to Yeats's visionary philosophy, and an Indian commentator might be allowed some insight into the poet's appropriation of Asian wisdom. Certainly George Orwell thought so, reviewing *The Development of W.B. Yeats* for *Horizon* (2005: 24). Later, he turns the spotlight on Orwell's review of what he calls 'a study from remoter parts' (2005: 380) by Menon, focusing in particular on Orwell's speculation on a possible link between Yeats's 'wayward, even tortured style of writing and his rather sinister vision of life' (2016 [1943]: 202). Highlighting that Orwell's review still haunts the scholarship, McCormack argues that this aspect 'remains as unanswered as it is unavoidable' and he asserts that 'its challenge surely begs an answer' (2005: 380). Although O'Brien is repeatedly referred to throughout McCormack's book, O'Brien's response, as we have seen, to Orwell on this issue is evidently disregarded by McCormack without comment.

Unusually, too, McCormack interrogates the finer meanings of Orwell's language and speculation: 'Yet what does he mean by "tendency"? Does he mean an inbuilt, ever-present bias… or does he mean something more active and less given, a thing responsive and changing…?' (2005: 380). McCormack adds that Orwell 'takes us further along a path of his unanswered questions', and then quotes Orwell's bombshell statements which, as we have also seen, are avoided by O'Brien: 'Translated into political terms, Yeats's tendency is Fascist. Throughout most of his life, and long before Fascism was ever heard of, he had had the outlook of those who reach Fascism by the aristocratic route' (2016 [1943]: 204). This leads into a rare critical reflection on the value and nature of Orwell's engagement with Menon's book:

> Given that Menon's endeavour was to gauge 'the great poetry of Yeats's last days' against *A Vision*, Orwell has most usefully turned the argument into a historical direction. Yeats's tendency preceded fascism, he says, without quite committing himself to the extreme view that the poet was a fascist *avant la lettre*. Instead, he discriminates between the various routes to fascism, Yeats having travelled on or close to the aristocratic one. Again, Orwell's caution is evident in his choice of words. For Yeats was no aristocrat, and could only have travelled *in the style* of one (2005: 380-381).

Although McCormack rightly discerns some caution in Orwell's approach in the *Horizon* review, this caution is less evident, as we shall see, in Orwell's subsequent *Time and Tide* review (April 1943) where he states matter-of-factly that Yeats had fascist sympathies. Moreover, McCormack's point on 'historical direction' is not quite fair to Menon, whose endeavour (as the book title indicates) was to study the development of Yeats across his oeuvre. The historical direction Menon sets up, in fact, in regard to Yeats's preceding aristocratic bias, germane to Yeats's later fascist leanings, is reaffirmed in the Conclusion to his book through his immense disquiet over Yeats's authoritarian attitude (under the influence of Pound in particular); his recognition that 'in a long-term objective analysis, poetry has played a great and necessary part in human history and the integration of human relationships' (1942: 93); his sense that judgment of 'such a towering figure as Yeats' should be easier after the war when 'the immediate problems which confront us are solved and our sense of values reintegrated' (ibid); and his consciously interim position pending the verdict of posterity:

> Until then one can only repeat the well-worn words that he was the last poet in the aristocratic tradition, and say that in his last days, with the bottom knocked out of his moral code, and unable to fully grasp the historical process, he fell back upon the pride and strength of the individual will, harping always on the type of nobility and greatness he had been brought up to accept. But his imaginative intensity never flagged, and everywhere his character and his personality stood out. Whatever the verdict of the future, his work will remain for ever the greatest personal document of our times (ibid).

McCormack later revisits the issue of a possible link between 'political tendency and literary style' (2005: 401). He provocatively draws a parallel between 'Yeats's staged decapitations and the brutalities of closed prison-camps' in the 1930s, and asserts: 'The challenge posed by Orwell and V. K. N. Menon remains unmet' (ibid). However, although McCormack rightly underscores both Orwell and Menon's enduring relevance to scrutiny of Yeats's politics, his engagement throughout is almost exclusively with the text of Orwell's review rather than Menon's book, too. Still, despite this shortcoming, the fact that he readily acknowledges Menon's seminal contribution (including highlighting Menon's Indian heritage as particularly beneficial to criticism of Yeats) and does not downplay or sever the connection between Orwell's review and Menon's book, could be seen to point towards a renewed sense of the importance of contextualisation in future scholarship. After all, while Menon's identity as the author of the Yeats book reviewed by Orwell is obviously no secret, and descriptions of him such as those by McCormack (for example, 'biographer-scholar' and 'Indian commentator') are sufficiently accurate, it remains that so little is widely known of who Menon was (in biographical and professional detail) whereas Orwell's life and works have been extensively covered by generations of biographers and critics. This huge disparity is not helped by quotation from Menon's book, if it occurs at all, tending to be via quotation from Orwell's review. Two issues are, therefore, sorely in need of scholarly attention: firstly, the lack of direct engagement with the text of Menon's book; and secondly, the lack of proper contextualisation of these two texts and writers, including reference to Orwell's subsequent review of Menon's book (in *Time and Tide*) and his broader professional relationship with Menon at the BBC.

A REMARKABLE MAN

As several volumes of *The Complete Works of George Orwell* (under the general editorship of Peter Davison) indicate in periodic fragments, the professional association between Orwell and Menon both predates and post-dates Orwell's first review of Menon's book (in *Horizon*, January 1943) by some time and is quite extensive. Volume XV, entitled *Two Wasted Years 1943* (1998), shows that there was even a role reversal. *Talking to India* (November 1943), 'which was published by George Allen & Unwin' and which Orwell 'edited and contributed to' (Davison 1998c: 320), was reviewed by Menon (*Tribune*, 26 May 1944) 'who had broadcast frequently for Orwell' (1998c: 324) at the BBC. Menon is also explicitly mentioned by Orwell in relation to the target audience in the Introduction, where he refers to 'a respectable number of Indian novelists and essayists (Ahmed Ali, Mulk Raj Anand, Cedric Dover and Narayana Menon, to name only four) who prefer to write in English' (1998c: 322). E. M. Forster, who endorsed Menon's book, was among the contributors: 'Author of *Howards End* and *A Passage to India*, etc' (1998c: 323). Although too copious to detail here, Orwell's BBC Indian Service-related correspondence includes, from 25 April 1942, dealing with frequent broadcast talks on literary and cultural topics and musical selections handled by Menon (who was a musician descended from musicians, as Grierson discloses in the Preface to Menon's book) as well as contracts for and payments to Menon for his broadcast contributions. In his note to Orwell's letter to 'Mr. Menon' dated 25 April 1942, in Volume XIII entitled *All Propaganda is Lies 1941-1942* (1998), Davison mentions that Menon later 'arranged Indian music (with S. Sinha) at the "Indian Demonstration" on 31 January 1943 at the London Coliseum' (2001 [1998a]: 285).

Mr or Dr Menon, as Orwell (or rather, Eric Blair) usually refers to him in the correspondence, was clearly a remarkable man: highly talented and competent, more than willing to co-operate with and assist Orwell, prepared to tackle diverse subjects (including at short notice), and duly described in glowing terms by Orwell to other correspondents – as 'gifted', for example, in a letter to Alex Comfort dated 13 July 1943 (Davison 1998c: 169). Some of the more notable events, in the context of their mutual interest in Yeats, were: a broadcast talk booked for Menon 'on the anti-Fascist Youth Rally' and 'Signed: Z. A. Bokhari' (Davison 2001 [1998b]: 29) in September 1942; a letter from Orwell to E. M. Forster about Menon's book in November 1942, suggesting it 'will, I think, be suitable to mention in your next talk' (Davison 2001 [1998b]: 182); and in December 1942, Menon's participation with, among others, Orwell and T. S. Eliot in the *Voice* radio magazine programme on the theme 'Oriental Influence on English Literature' (Davison 2001 [1998b]: 211), which featured several poems by Yeats.

Furthermore, Orwell saw fit to review Menon's book a second time. His lesser known review for *Time and Tide* (17 April 1943) adopts a more straightforward and conversational approach (including a humorous reference to Yeats's occult beliefs as 'yogey-bogey') and comes across as more admiring of Yeats the poet despite being highly critical, again, of Yeats's occult preoccupations and political leanings (Orwell 1998 [1943]: 71). Orwell commences by focusing on the 'three main phases' of Yeats's development and works up to an excoriating portrayal of Yeats's hatred 'of the modern world', 'the democratic, rationalistic outlook' and 'the concept of human equality', highlighting the occult elements and ominous implications of *A Vision* (1998 [1943]: 70). Orwell states matter-of-factly that Yeats was 'sympathetic towards Fascism, at least the Italian version of it', reiterating the influence on Yeats of 'Ezra Pound and various Italian thinkers' but also that Yeats might not have followed, ultimately, in the direction of Pound (ibid). Nevertheless, Orwell discharges a highly explosive statement: Yeats's 'The Second Coming' (1920) does not imply disapproval, he says, even though 'the rise of the Nazis seems to be foretold' (ibid). Notably, Orwell distinguishes to a greater degree between Yeats's politics and literary achievement: 'As Mr Menon rightly says, Yeats's acceptance of Fascism is a "disquieting symptom", but it in no way detracts from the interest of his literary development' (1998 [1943]: 70-71). As a result, Orwell concludes with high praise for – rather than, as in the first review, a chilling warning about – Yeats's writings, and once again approves of Menon's study: '[Yeats's] life was devoted to poetry with a completeness that has been very rare among the English-speaking peoples, and the results justified it. In spite of some patches of absurdity it is an impressive story, and Mr Menon retells it with great delicacy and acuteness' (1998 [1943]: 71).

The overall relation between Orwell and Menon, then, is much broader in its scope and more complex in its details than scholars, in the main, have cared to research and report. Instead, for many years, Orwell's first review has been largely prioritised at the expense of Menon's book in regard to the debate over Yeats's alleged fascist leanings. Therefore, this paper calls for a change to this unsatisfactory state of affairs through reinstatement of Menon's book to its due level of importance as both the precursor to and subject of Orwell's reviews. This level of importance Orwell himself clearly respected. It is incumbent on scholars to rebalance critical treatment of, and thus to reconnect, these texts through enhanced contextualisation in a suitably unified rather than fragmentary manner. This will require greater recognition and appreciation of both writers as a) key instigators of, and contributors to, what is still an ongoing debate concerning Yeats and fascism, and b) professional associates at the BBC.

Moreover, hopefully further biographical and professional details could be ascertained beyond Menon's work with Orwell for the BBC and Menon's book on Yeats (in which he is referred to, on the title page, as 'Senior Carnegie Scholar in English at the University of Edinburgh' and which, according to Davison on p. 289 of Volume XIV, is the only book by Menon listed in the British Library). While images of Orwell have proliferated in the scholarship and, in the 21st century, on social media, many scholars are likely to have never seen an image of Menon to know what he even looked like. A BBC blog by Professor James Procter, entitled 'The Empire Scripts Back' and dated 26 October 2018, contains a shadowy black-and-white BBC group photograph from December 1942 which includes 'BBC music producer Narayana Menon' (Procter 2018), amusingly on the far right, as well as Orwell and T. S. Eliot. As Menon's side profile and obscured features seem aptly to suggest, there was certainly more to the mysterious Dr Menon than meets the eye. Scholarship that expressly illuminates, so to speak, who Menon was and what he achieved in his life and career would be a long overdue and, surely, welcome development in Orwell studies.

REFERENCES

Allt, Peter and Alspach, Russell K. (eds) (1957) *The Variorum Edition of the Poems of W. B. Yeats*, New York: The Macmillan Company

Bloom, Harold (1975 [1973]) *The Anxiety of Influence: A Theory of Poetry*, Oxford: Oxford University Press

Cullingford, Elizabeth (1984 [1981]) *Yeats, Ireland and Fascism*, London: The Macmillan Press Ltd

Davison, Peter (ed.) (2001 [1998a]) *Collected Works of George Orwell, Vol. XIII: All Propaganda is Lies 1941-1942*, London: Secker & Warburg

Davison, Peter (ed.) (2001 [1998b]) *Collected Works of George Orwell, Vol. XIV: Keeping Our Little Corner Clean 1942-1943*, London: Secker & Warburg

Davison, Peter (ed.) (1998c) *Collected Works of George Orwell, Vol. XV: Two Wasted Years 1943*, London: Secker & Warburg

Foster, R. F. (2003) *W. B. Yeats: A Life II. The Arch-Poet 1915-1939*, Oxford: Oxford University Press

Freyer, Grattan (1981) *W. B. Yeats and the Anti-Democratic Tradition*, Dublin: Gill and Macmillan Ltd

Jeffares, A. N. and Knowland, A. S. (eds) (1975) *A Commentary on the Collected Plays of W. B. Yeats*, Stanford: Stanford University Press

MacNeice, Louis (1941) *The Poetry of W. B. Yeats*, Oxford: Oxford University Press

McCormack, W. J. (2005) *Blood Kindred: W. B. Yeats – The Life, The Death, The Politics*, London: Pimlico (Random House)

McGarry, Fearghal (2005) *Eoin O'Duffy: A Self-Made Hero*, Oxford: Oxford University Press

Menon, V. K. Narayana (1942) *The Development of William Butler Yeats*, Edinburgh: Oliver and Boyd

Menon, V. K. Narayana (1960 [1942]) *The Development of William Butler Yeats*, Edinburgh: Oliver and Boyd, second edition

O'Brien, Conor Cruise (1988 [1965]) *Passion & Cunning: Essays on Nationalism, Terrorism & Revolution*, New York: Simon & Schuster

Orwell, George (2016 [1943]) Review: V. K. Narayana Menon, *The Development of William Butler Yeats*, Davison, Peter (ed.) *George Orwell: Seeing Things as They Are: Selected Journalism and Other Writings*, London: Penguin Books pp 202-207

Orwell, George (1998 [1943]) Review of *The Development of William Butler Yeats* by V. K. Narayana Menon, Davison, Peter (ed.) (1998c) *Collected Works of George Orwell, Vol. XV: Two Wasted Years 1941-1943*, London: Secker & Warburg pp 69-71

Procter, James (2018) The Empire scripts back, bbc.co.uk, 26 October. Available online at https://www.bbc.co.uk/blogs/bbchistoryresearch/entries/75ecb85c-7c40-4eca-b9bb-8e5f5195ce70, accessed on 20 September 2020

Tompsett, Daniel (2018) *Unlocking the Poetry of W. B. Yeats: Heart Mysteries*, New York: Routledge

Wade, Allan (1954) *The Letters of W. B. Yeats*, London: Rupert Hart-Davis

White, Terence de Vere (1966) *Kevin O'Higgins*, Dublin: Anvil Press

Yeats, W. B. (2008 [1926]) *A Vision* (dated 1925, published 1926) Paul, Catherine E. and Harper, Margaret Mills (eds) *The Collected Works of W. B. Yeats: Volume XIII*, New York: Scribner

JARON MURPHY

Yeats, W. B. (1990 [1937]) *A Vision* (1937, revised edition) Jeffares, A. Norman (ed.) *W. B. Yeats: A Vision and Related Writings*. London: Arena (Arrow Books Limited)

NOTE ON THE CONTRIBUTOR

Dr Jaron Murphy holds a DPhil in English Language and Literature from the University of Oxford and currently teaches across the undergraduate and postgraduate Multimedia Journalism and Communication courses at Bournemouth University. An award-winning journalist, he recently appeared on the UK National Council for the Training of Journalists (NCTJ) list of most respected journalists following research by Cardiff University. Dr Murphy is also a member of the Orwell Society.

PAPER

Orwell, Advertisements and the Political Economy of the Media

RICHARD LANCE KEEBLE

George Orwell, throughout his career as a novelist and journalist, maintained a fascination with advertisements that has been largely missed in the many studies of his life and writings. This focus on advertisements ties in particular with the political economy approach he adopts in his analyses of the operations and content of newspapers and magazines – and with his interests in propaganda and language. Orwell is interested in the ways advertisements reflect the politics and financial status of media consumers – and he often sees the quirky and the humorous in his analyses of ads. This paper examines critically his comments on advertisements dotted about his diaries, in his 'state of the nation' essays, in his 'As I Please' columns in the leftist journal, Tribune, *in the 'London Letters' he composes for the American journal,* Partisan Review *– and in his novel* Keep the Aspidistra Flying *(1936) where the world of advertising features so prominently and symbolically. His fascination with the political function of advertising culminates in his depiction of the propaganda posters in the Big Brother world of his dystopian masterpiece* Nineteen Eighty-Four *(1949) – published just days before his untimely death at 46..*

ADVERTISING AND THE MYTH OF MEDIA FREEDOM

Throughout all his writings on the press Orwell maintains a consistent 'political economy' approach, questioning the notion of press freedom, stressing the impact of advertisers and proprietorial control on content – and highlighting the close integration of mainstream newspapers with dominant financial, political and military interests and their essential propaganda role for the wealthy.

Significantly, his first published piece in the UK, 'A farthing newspaper' (for Chesterton's review *G. K's Weekly*) adopts a political economy approach that he is to maintain throughout his writing career (Orwell 1970 [1928]: 34-37). *Ami du Peuple*, costing just ten centimes, has recently been launched in Paris with a manifesto claiming it is 'uncontaminated by any base thoughts of gain' (ibid: 34). Blair adds, ironically:

RICHARD LANCE KEEBLE

The proprietors, who hide their blushes in anonymity, are emptying their pockets for the mere pleasure of doing good by stealth. Their objects, we learn, are to make war on the great trusts, to fight for a lower cost of living and above all combat the powerful newspapers which are strangling free speech in France (ibid: 34-35).

He proceeds to deconstruct, with polemical vigour, the paper's pretensions – noting that its proprietor is M. Coty 'a great industrial capitalist and also proprietor of the *Figaro* and the *Gaulois*'. In other words, it is merely putting across 'the sort of propaganda wanted by M. Coty and his associates' (see Dulley 2015: 16-17).

Underlying Orwell's comments on the press throughout his career (from that early essay on *Ami du Peuple*, of 1928, onwards) is a desire to highlight the economic factors impacting on its operations and political bias. For instance, in *The Lion and the Unicorn* (1970 [1941a]), written during some of the bleakest days of the Second World War when Britain seriously feared invasion by the Nazis, he writes bluntly: 'Is the English press honest or dishonest? At normal times it is deeply dishonest. All the papers that matter live off their advertisements and the advertisers exercise an indirect censorship over news' (ibid: 88).

Orwell now returns to his long-standing, political economy critique, highlighting the impact of advertising and proprietorial monopolies on press content:

> The unbearable silliness of English newspapers from about 1900 onwards has two main causes. One is that nearly the whole of the press is in the hands of a few big capitalists who are interested in the continuance of capitalism and therefore in preventing the public from learning to think: the other is that in peacetime newspapers live off advertisements for consumption goods, building societies, cosmetics and the like and are therefore interested in maintaining a 'sunshine mentality' which will induce people to spend money. … Therefore, don't let people know the facts about the political and economic situation; divert their attention to giant pandas, channel swimmers, royal weddings and other soothing topics (ibid).

In one of the 'London Letters' he contributes to the American leftist journal, *Partisan Review*, in 1941, he says he has detected a change in tone of the popular press which have become 'politically serious while preserving their "stunt" make-up with screaming headlines etc' (Orwell 1970 [1941b]: 137-138).

And detailed observations on advertisements feature in his 'London Letter' for the November-December 1942. He writes:

One periodical reminder that things *have changed* in England since the war is the arrival of American magazines, with their enormous bulk, sleek paper and riot of brilliantly coloured adverts urging you to spend your money on trash. English adverts before the war were no doubt less colourful and enterprising than the American ones, but their mental atmosphere was similar, and the sight of a full-page ad on shiny paper gives one the sensation of stepping back into 1939. ... An extraordinary feature of the time is advertisements for products which no longer exist. To give just one example: the word IRON in large letters, with underneath it an impressive picture of a tank, and underneath that a little essay on the importance of collecting scrap iron for salvage; at the bottom, in tiny print, a reminder that after the war Iron Jelloids will be on sale as before (Orwell 1970 [1942]: 270-271; italics in the original).

He then moves on to consider much broader, complex issues such as workers' attitudes to the war and the future of capitalism, no less. So he highlights the 'strange fact' – recently reported by the Mass Observers and confirmed by his own limited experience – that many factory workers are actually afraid of the war ending since they foresee a return to the old conditions with three million unemployed etc. He continues:

PAPER

The idea that *whatever happens* old-style capitalism is doomed and we are in much more danger of forced labour than of unemployment, hasn't reached the masses except as a vague notion that 'things will be different' (ibid: 271; italics in the original).

He next returns to the main theme observing: 'The advertisements that have been least changed by the war are those of theatres and patent medicines' (ibid).

Orwell's preoccupation with advertising often crops up in unlikely places. For instance, he begins a long review essay on *Beggar my Neighbour*, by Lionel Fielden, for *Horizon*, September 1943, reprinted in *Partisan Review*, in the Winter 1944 edition, with this somewhat idiosyncratic comment:

If you compare commercial advertising with political propaganda, one thing that strikes you is its relative intellectual honesty. The advertiser at least knows what he is aiming at – that is, money – whereas the propagandist, when he is not a lifeless hack, is often a neurotic working off some private grudge and actually desirous of the exact opposite of the thing he advocates (Orwell 1970 [1943]: 349).

RICHARD LANCE KEEBLE

THE PLEASURE OF ANALYSING ADS

In 1943, Orwell quits as Talks Producer for the Eastern Service after two largely unhappy years at the BBC and becomes literary editor of the leftist journal *Tribune*. As part of his role, between 1943 and 1947 he composes 80 weekly 'As I Please' columns. And his preoccupations with many aspects of advertising are regularly given full rein.

In an 'As I Please' column in 1944, he focuses yet again on the subject of advertising, suggesting that, during the war, the 'advertiser has temporarily lost his grip' and so newspapers 'are far more intelligent than they were five years ago' (Orwell 1998 [1944a]: 146). 'At the same time there has been an increase in censorship and official interference, but this is not nearly so crippling and not nearly so conducive to sheer silliness. It is better to be controlled by bureaucrats than by common swindlers' (ibid). His unrelenting critique continues:

> Most newspapers remain completely reckless about details of fact. The belief that what is 'in the papers' must be true has been gradually evaporating ever since Northcliffe set out to vulgarise journalism, and the war has not yet arrested the process. Many people frankly say that they take in such and such a paper because it is lively but that they don't believe a word of what it says (ibid).

Orwell even examines – originally and with great wit – the links between advertising, government propaganda and a short story in *Home Companion and Family Journal* (possibly purchased by his wife, Eileen Blair, and left about their flat in Mortimer Crescent, London NW6l) in an 'As I Please' column of 25 February 1944. The story, he notes, tells of the adventures of a young girl named Lucy Fallows who works on the switchboard of a long-distance telephone exchange. Her job, normally boring, suddenly livens up and she finds herself in the midst of thrilling adventures involving the sinking of a U-boat, the capture of a German sabotage crew and a long motorcycle ride with a handsome naval officer (Orwell 1998 [1944b]: 103). At the end, there is this short note:

> Any of our young readers themselves interested in the work of the Long Distance Telephone Exchange … should apply to the Staff Controller, L. T. R., London, who will inform them as to the opportunities open (ibid).

This sets Orwell off on an extraordinary creative riff. First he questions whether the advertisement will have any success: 'I should doubt whether even girls of the age aimed at would believe that capturing U-boats enters very largely into the lives of telephone operators.' But he notes, 'with interest', 'the direct correlation between a Government recruiting advertisement and a piece of commercial fiction'. Such stories are probably not written to order; rather, the departments concerned keep their eye on the weekly papers and 'push in an ad. when any story seems likely to form an attractive bait'. Orwell relishes in the absurdity of it all: he imagines 'some stripe-trousered personage in the GPO reading "Hullo, Sweetheart" as part of his official duties'. Next he imagines this hilarious dialogue:

> 'Hullo, Hullo. Is that you, Tony? Oh, hullo. Look here, I've got another script for you, Tony, "A Ticket to Paradise". It's bus conductresses this time. They are not coming in. I believe the trousers don't fit, or something. Well, any way, Peter says make it sexy, but kind of clean – *you* know. Nothing extramarital. We want the stuff in by Tuesday. Fifteen thousand words. You can choose the hero. I rather favour the kind of outdoor man that dogs and kiddies all love him – you know. Or very tall with a sensitive mouth. I don't mind really. But pile on the sex, Peter says' (ibid: 103-104).

Orwell ends this opening section of the column in a reflective mood, moving from the specific and seemingly trivial to the more general and important cultural/political issue: 'Something resembling this already happens with radio features and documentary films, but hitherto there has not been any very direct connection between fiction and propaganda. That half-inch in the *Home Companion* seems to mark another small stage in the process of "co-ordination" that is gradually happening to all the arts.'

Incidentally, on 10 March, *Tribune* published a note from the editor of *Home Companion* saying the magazine received 'no payment or other consideration' from the GPO or any other government department for publishing the note. Orwell, as ever keen to engage with his readers, says he never suggested that the Amalgamated Press received payment for publishing the story, but if he seemed to imply this he apologises. He continues: 'I would still like to know, however, who was responsible for inserting the "little note" and for its precise wording, with instructions as to where to apply for a job' (ibid: 105).

In another 'As I Please' column on 9 June 1944, Orwell highlights (with almost venomous fury) the ways in which the proprietorial and advertiser control of the press impacts even on the content of literary reviews and what he describes as 'the book racket' (Orwell 1998 [1944c]: 251-253):

> The literary papers of several well-known papers were practically owned by a handful of publishers who had their quislings planted in all the important jobs. These wretches churned forth

RICHARD LANCE KEEBLE

their praise – 'masterpiece', 'brilliant', 'unforgettable' and so forth – like so many mechanical pianos. A book coming from the right publishers could be absolutely certain not only of favourable reviews, but of being placed on the 'recommended' list which industrious book-borrowers would cut out and take to the library the next day (ibid: 251-252).

On the power of advertisers, he writes: 'A book coming from a big publisher, who habitually spent large sums on advertisement, might get fifty or seventy-five reviews: a book from a small publisher might get only twenty' (ibid: 252).

Next, reading *Old Moore's Almanac* reminds him of the fun and games he had as a youth somewhat mischievously answering advertisements. In his 'As I Please' column on 24 November 1944, he lists – with evident relish – advertisements 'some of which have remained totally unchanged for at least thirty years': 'Increase your height, earn five pounds a week in your spare time, drink habit conquered in three days, electric belts, bust developers and cures for obesity, insomnia, bunions, backache, red noses, stammering, blushing, piles, bad legs, flat feet and baldness' (ibid: 472).

Many years ago, he says, he answered an advertisement from Winifred Grace Hartland who undertook to cure obesity. She replied – assuming him to be a woman – urging him to come and see her at once. 'Do come,' she writes, 'before ordering your summer frocks, as after taking my course your figure would have altered out of all recognition.' Orwell continues, revelling in the deception:

> She was particularly insistent that I should make a personal visit and gave an address somewhere in London Docks. This went on for a long time, during which the fee gradually sank from two guineas to half a crown, and then I brought the matter to an end by writing to say that I had been cured of my obesity by a rival agency (ibid).

He adds that later the magazine *Truth* revealed there was no such person as Winifred Grace Hartland; rather it was a swindle run by two American crooks, Harry Sweet and Dave Little. And Orwell ends this section, wittily, rather quirkily and with a pinch of schoolboyish 'naughtiness': 'It is curious they should have been so anxious for a personal visit, and indeed I have since wondered whether Harry Sweet and Dave Little were actually engaged in shipping consignments of fat women to the harems of Istanbul' (ibid: 473).

Orwell returns to the issue in his 17 November 1944 column. The proprietors have sent him the current issue of the *Writer* which he had wrongly stated earlier as being defunct. He is happy to correct himself, but goes on to examine the advertisements of people selling their journalism training services. One, for instance, reads: 'Plotting without tears. Learn my way. The simplest method ever. Money returned if dissatisfied. 5 shillings post free' (Orwell 1998 {1944d}: 464). Orwell comments with merciless wit: isn't it curious that the trainers are rarely well-known writers? 'If Bernard Shaw or J. B. Priestley offered to teach you how to make money out of writing, you might feel that there was something in it. But who would buy a bottle of hair restorer from a bald man?' (ibid).

Orwell constantly and deliberately subverts the expectations of his readers – moving his attention to ever-changing, surprisingly original topics. Thus, his 'As I Please' column, on 8 November 1946, begins: 'Someone has just sent me a copy of an American fashion magazine which shall be nameless' (Orwell 1998 [1946a]: 471). In fact, it was *Vogue*, which had been posted to his London address because, amongst its many photographs of glamorous women, was a profile of Orwell. So he proceeds to deconstruct the magazine, noting: 'One striking thing when one looks at these pictures is the overbred, exhausted, even decadent style of beauty that now seems to be striven after. Nearly all of these women are immensely elongated.' On the prose style of the advertisements, he says it's 'an extraordinary mixture of sheer lushness with clipped and sometimes very expressive technical jargon'. And, typically, Orwell focuses on what's missing: 'A fairly diligent search through the magazine reveals two discreet allusions to grey hair, but if there is anywhere a direct mention of fatness or middle age I have not found it. Birth and death are not mentioned either: nor is work, except that a few recipes for breakfast dishes as given' (ibid).

Another intriguing way of critiquing the press and highlighting the crucial function of advertisements appears in the 'As I Please' column on 22 November 1946. Here Orwell simply presents two lists and subjects them to 'ironic reversal', as Alex Woloch points out (2016: 246): one shows major newspapers in order of intelligence (*Manchester Guardian, Times, News Chronicle, Telegraph, Herald, Mail, Mirror, Express, Graphic*); the other in order of popularity (*Express, Herald, Mirror, News Chronicle, Mail, Graphic, Telegraph, Times, Manchester Guardian*). He comments (Orwell 1998 [1946b]: 500): 'It will be seen that the second list is very nearly – not quite, for life is never so neat as that – the first turned upside down.' For Orwell, the solution lies in the alternative press: 'In these circumstances it is difficult to foresee a radical change, even if the special kind of pressure exerted by owners and advertisers is removed. What matters is that in England we do possess juridical liberty of the Press, which makes it possible to utter one's true opinions fearlessly in papers of comparatively small circulation' (ibid).

RICHARD LANCE KEEBLE

ADVERTISING – THE 'RATTLING OF A STICK INSIDE A SWILL-BUCKET'

Advertising plays a crucial role both symbolically and in the narrative of Orwell's novel *Keep the Aspidistra Flying* (1976 [1936]: 573-737). As Gordon Bowker argues, it is a novel bursting with Rabelaisian gaiety and high spirits (2003: 171) and ads become a focus for Orwell's ironic banter and mischievous wordplay – as well as his critique of Americanised capitalism.

Gordon Comstock, the anti-hero, is a poverty-stricken aspiring poet belonging to 'the most dismal of all classes, the middle-middle class, the landed gentry' (op cit: 598). When we first meet him he is working at Mr McKechnie's bookshop. Significantly, the streets around it are completely taken over by advertisements:

> Opposite, next to the Prince of Wales, were tall hoardings covered with ads for patent foods and patent medicines. A gallery of monstrous doll-faces – pink vacuous faces, full of goofy optimism. Q. T. Sauce, Truweet Breakfast Crisps ('Kiddies clamour for their Breakfast Crisps'), Kangaroo Burgundy, Vitamalt Chocolate, Bovex. Of them all, the Bovex one oppressed Gordon the most. A spectacle rat-faced clerk, with patent-leather hair, sitting at a café table grinning over a white mug of Bovex. 'Corner Table enjoys his meal with Bovex', the legend ran (ibid: 578).

Gordon's eyes remain fixed on the advertisements that inspire a kind of poetic flourish: 'The poster that advertised Q. T. Sauce was torn at the edge, a ribbon of paper fluttered fitfully like a tiny pennant' (ibid: 579). He struggles with the first two lines of a new poem. Orwell continues: 'His eyes refocused themselves on the posters opposite. He had his private reasons for hating them. Mechanically he re-read their slogans. 'Kangaroo Burgundy – the wine for Britons.' 'Asthma was choking her.' 'Q. T. Sauce Keep Hubby Smiling' … (ibid).

In another interval between dealing with his bookshop customers, Gordon again looks at the ads.

> He really hated them this time. That Vitamalt one, for instance. 'Hike all day on a slab of Vitamalt.' A youthful couple, boy and girl, in clean-minded hiking kit, their hair picturesquely tousled by the wind, climbing a stile against a Sussex landscape. That girl's face. The awful bright tomboy cheeriness of it. The kind of girl who goes in for Plenty of Clean Fun. Windswept. Tight khaki shorts but that doesn't mean you can pinch her backside. And next to them – Corner Table. 'Corner Table enjoys his meal with Bovex.' Gordon examined the thing with the intimacy of hatred. The idiotic grinning face, like the face of a self-satisfied rat, the slick black hair, the silly spectacles… (ibid: 584-585).

When Gordon next looks at the ads he associates them with the 'sense of disintegration, of decay, that is endemic in our time' (ibid: 586). 'He looked now with more seeing eyes at those grinning yard-wide faces. After all, there was more than mere silliness, greed and vulgarity. Corner Table grins at you, seemingly optimistic, with a flash of false teeth. But what is behind the grin? Desolation, emptiness, prophesies of doom.'

Given Gordon's hatred of the world of advertising, it is somewhat ironic that he suddenly acquires a job in the accounts department of the New Albion Publicity Company – through a 'friend of a friend' of his lady friend's employer's brother, as Orwell explains, highlighting subtly and wittily the ways in which nepotism plays such a crucial role in the operations of capitalism. New Albion 'designed a certain number of large-scale posters for oatmeal stout, self-raising flour, and so forth, but its main line was millinery and cosmetic advertisements in the women's illustrated papers, besides minor ads in twopenny weeklies, such as Whiterose Pills for Female Disorders, Your Horoscope Cast by Professor Raratonga, The Seven Secrets of Venus, New Hope for the Ruptured, Earn Five Pounds a Week in your Spare Time, and Cyprolax Hair Lotion Banishes all Unpleasant Intruders' (ibid: 607-608). Lists always hold a fascination for Orwell and it is clear here how he relishes piling on the details of the silly slogans one after another.

The outraged, obsessive voices of the narrator and Gordon next come together to condemn advertising as nothing less than 'the dirtiest ramp' of modern, American-style capitalism. 'Most of the employees were hard-boiled, Americanized, go-getting type to whom nothing in the world is sacred, except money. They had their cynical code worked out. The public are swine; advertising is the rattling of a stick inside a swill-bucket. And yet beneath their cynicism there was the final naïveté, the blind worship of the money-god' (ibid: 608).

In the course of the novel, Gordon quits his job at New Albion, pursues Rosemary, gets drunk, and ends up in a police cell – only for his aristocratic editor friend Ravelston (modelled on Orwell's friend, Sir Richard Rees) to pay the fine. After all that, Gordon returns to work at the bookshop. But then when Rosemary becomes pregnant they reject the idea of an abortion and decide to wed and settle for a life a respectability – complete with an aspidistra in their flat off the Edgware Road. Symbolic of this retreat to bourgeois life (previously condemned in the novel for its stultifying emptiness and deadness), is Gordon's return to New Albion. In no time, he is promoted to work alongside a Mr Clew writing ads for a new deodorant produced by the Queen of Sheba Toilet Requisites Co. 'Gordon watched his own development, first with surprise, then with amusement and finally with a kind of horror. *This*, then, was what he was coming to. Writing lies to tickle the money out of fools' packets' (ibid: 609, italics in the original). He even invents a slogan: 'P. P.'

Orwell has an enormous amount of fun throughout the novel playing with the language he uses to evoke the world of advertising. The New Albion Publicity Co. is the actual name of the firm run by the father of one of his friends, Michael Sayer, and Orwell is clearly pleased to have slipped that past his publishers. When Gordon meets Rosemary for the first time, he strokes her face in the night-time darkness and quotes four lines in medieval French (attributed to Villon). When Rosemary asks him to translate he does so. In fact, it's a subtle invitation to *fellatio*. Not surprisingly Rosemary refuses – despite Gordon's persistent pleas for her to satisfy him. So again, Orwell has had fun deceiving the censor. Another Orwellian joke is the name he gives his anti-hero – for Comstock (1844-1915) was a notorious anti-vice campaigner in the States who opposed abortion, prostitution, gambling and contraception (see Bowker 2003: 171; Werbel 2018). He even enjoys playing around with the slogan 'P. P.' – exposing at the same time both the cynicism and naïveté of the advertisers and the gullibility of the public. It stands for Pedic Perspiration. 'Gordon had searched for the word pedic in the Oxford Dictionary and found it did not exist. But Mr Warner [his boss] has said Hell what did it matter anyway? It would put the wind up them just the same' (ibid: 734). But what Orwell enjoys most of all is the fact that, in French, 'peepee' is slang for piss.

Yet Daphne Patai (1984: 113) rightly identifies the appalling sexism that underlies Orwell's representation of the advertising industry. For it is women who are blamed for luring men from the path of social justice into the seductive arms of consumerism. Significantly, most of the adverts Gordon either sees or works on are directed principally at women. As Gordon rants:

> Every man you can see has got some blasted woman hanging round his neck like a mermaid, dragging him down and down – down to some beastly little semi-detached villa in Putney, with hire-purchase furniture and a portable radio and an aspidistra in the window. … A woman's got a sort of mystical feeling towards money. Good and evil in a woman's mind mean simply money and no money' (op cit: 649).

Patai comments: 'As ridiculous as Gordon's comments sound in their evasion of any serious consideration of women, men, and money, they are given some plausibility by the narrative focus, which allows Gordon to speak while giving Rosemary no serious argument in return. She simply laughs at him in a conciliatory and good-natured way' (op cit: 114).

THE JOURNALS – AND THE CONSTANT INTEREST IN ADS

Orwell's fascination with advertisements is particularly evident in many of his diary entries. From September 1938 to March 1939, the Blairs took a break in Marrakesh – paid for by an anonymous donor. Orwell had just spent six months in a sanatorium recovering from a serious health crisis, had been diagnosed with TB and was advised by his doctors to stay awhile in a hotter climate; Eileen Blair was exhausted and also needed a holiday (Topp 2020: 224-234). While in the Moroccan capital, Orwell, still not in the best of health, still managed to read extensively, to complete his novel *Coming Up for Air* (1939) and the wonderfully original essay on Dickens (to be published in his essay collection, *Inside the Whale*, in 1940) – and to write many letters and diary entries.

On 22 December 1938, he takes the time to note: 'The other widely read French weekly paper is *Gringoire*. Used to be a sort of gossipy literary paper but now much as *Candide*. I notice that those papers, though evidently prosperous and having a lot of advertisements, are not above inserting pornographic advertisements' (Orwell 2010: 118).

PAPER

Back in England, he maintains a regular wartime diary. For the entry on 6 June 1940, he conducts a 'rough analysis' of the advertisements in that day's edition of the *People*. So with a meticulous attention to detail, he conducts a quantitative survey: 'Paper consists of 12 pages – 84 columns. Of this just about 26 and a half columns (over one quarter) is advertisements. These are divided up as follows: *Food and drink* 5 and three quarters columns. *Patent medicines* 9 and a third. *Tobacco* 1. *Gambling* 2 and a third. *Clothes* 1 and a half. *Miscellaneous* 6 and three quarters' (ibid: 249, italics in the original). He concludes:

> Of 9 food and drink adverts, 6 are for unnecessary luxuries. Of 29 adverts for medicines, 19 are for things which are either fraudulent (baldness cured) more or less deleterious (Kruschen Salts, Bile Beans etc) or of the blackmail type ('Your child's stomach needs magnesia'). Benefit of doubt has been allowed in the case of a few medicines. Of 14 miscellaneous adverts, 4 are for soap, 1 for cosmetics, 1 for a holiday resort and 2 are government advertisements, including a large one for national savings. On 3 adverts in all classes are cashing in on the war (ibid: 249-250).

A few days later, on 6 June, he records seeing a huge advert on the side of a bus: 'FIRST AID IN WARTIME, FOR HEALTH, STRENGTH AND FORTITUDE. WRIGLEY'S CHEWING GUM' (ibid: 250). And the next day he reflects:

RICHARD LANCE KEEBLE

Although newspaper posters are now suppressed, one fairly frequently sees the paper-sellers displaying a poster. It appears that old ones are resuscitated and used and one with captions like 'RAF raids on Germany' or 'Enormous German losses' can be used at almost all times (ibid: 250-251).

On 13 June, he draws from his experience fighting with a Republican militia during the Spanish civil in 1937 to comment: 'I notice that one of the posters recruiting for the Pioneers, of a foot treading on a swastika with the legend "Step on it" is cribbed from a Government poster of the Spanish war, i.e. cribbed as to the idea. Of course, it is vulgarised and made comic but its appearance at any rate shows that the Government are beginning to be willing to learn' (ibid: 253). His preoccupation with the crucial propaganda function of advertisements within a capitalist economy of mindless consumption continues the following day with this entry which is bursting with moral outrage:

> Always as I walk through the Underground stations, sickened by the advertisements, the silly staring faces and strident colours, the general frantic struggle to induce people to waste labour and material by consuming useless luxuries or harmful drugs. How much rubbish this war will sweep away, if only we can hang on throughout the summer. War is simply the reversal of civilised life, its motto is 'Evil be thou my good' [a quotation from Milton's *Paradise Lost*], and so much of the good of modern life is actually evil that it is questionable whether on balance war does harm (ibid: 254).

Orwell returns to his long-standing political economy critique of the press and the underlying myth of media freedom in his entry for 29 June: '… the "freedom" of the press really means it depends on vested interests and largely (though its advertisements) on the luxury trades. Newspapers which would resist direct treachery can't take a strong line about cutting down luxuries when they live by advertising chocolates and silk stockings' (ibid: 265).

And just as during his youth he enjoyed responding mischievously to advertisements by assuming false identities, here he is clearly amused by an advert in pub for pick-me-up tablets called, of all things, Blitz. So, with meticulous attention to detail and, once again, indulging his likeness for listing, he simply reproduces the ad, line by line:

> Thoroughly recommended by the
> Medical Profession
> The
> 'LIGHTNING'

Marvellous discovery
Millions take this remedy
for
Hangover
War Nerves
Influenza
Headache
Toothache
Neuralgia
Sleeplessness
Rheumatism
Depression etc etc
Contains no Aspirin.

FROM CONSUMERISM TO BIG BROTHER PROPAGANDA IN *NINETEEN EIGHTY-FOUR*

Just as the streets in Gordon Comstock's London of *Keep the Aspidistra Flying* are dominated by advertising hoardings, so posters are everywhere in the London roads of Winston Smith's *Nineteen Eighty-Four* (2000 [1949]). At the start of the novel, Winston walks from his flat in Victory Mansions and looks around:

> Down in the street little eddies of wind were whirling dust and torn paper into spirals, and though the sun was shining and the sky a harsh blue, there seemed to be no colour in anything, except the posters that were plastered everywhere. The black-moustachio'd face gazed down from every commanding corner. There was one on the house-front immediately opposite. BIG BROTHER IS WATCHING YOU, the caption said, while the dark eyes looked deep into Winston's eyes. Down at street level another poster, torn at one corner, flapped fitfully in the wind, alternately covering and uncovering the single word INGSOC (ibid: 4).

And the slogans on posters at the Ministry of Love and on telescreens everywhere no longer focus on tempting people to spend, spend, spend; rather they spell out the principles of the Party: 'WAR IS PEACE/FREEDOM IS SLAVERY/IGNORANCE IS STRENGTH' (ibid: 6; 19).

So the messages have changed: the consumerist capitalism of *Keep the Aspidistra Flying* has given way to the authoritarian propaganda of the surveillance, hyper-militarised state.

Moreover, the abuse of language which Orwell has detected in the advertising industry culminates in his representation of newspeak and doublespeak in the novel. Emmanuel Goldstein's *The Theory and Practice of Oligarchical Collectivism* – the dissident tract which Winston reads to his lover, Julia, in their hideaway above Charrington's junk shop – 'means the power of holding two contradictory beliefs in one's mind simultaneously and accepting both of them. ... *Doublethink* lies at the very heart of Ingsoc [the Party's ideology], since the essential act of the Party is to use conscious deception while retaining the firmness of purpose that goes with complete honesty' (ibid: 244, italics in the original). Newspeak, on the other, is the official language of the state, its structure and etymology outlined in an Appendix at the end of the novel. Just as advertisements use short, snappy, hyper-simplified phrases to appeal to the consumerist mind-set, so Newspeak involves the actual destruction of words. So, for instance, the Ministry of Love becomes Miniluv; the Ministry of Peace becomes Minipax, and so on (ibid: 6). WAR IS PEACE and the other Party propaganda slogans displayed everywhere are, then, the consummate embodiments of doublethink and Newspeak.

CONCLUSIONS

Orwell's interest in advertisements was constant throughout his career as a writer and shows up prominently in his journalism, diary entries and novels. How strange that it has been largely missed by his biographers. He is extraordinarily inventive in his approach: in his diary, he conducts a laborious, meticulous, quantitative analysis of the advertising content of one issue of the *People* newspaper; in his 'As I Please' columns in *Tribune* he tackles the topic so originally and with such humour, highlighting, for instance, the subtle intrusion of government publicity in (of all places) a short story in *Home Companion and Family Journal*. That verve and wit also appear in his approach to advertisements in his novel, *Keep the Aspidistra Flying*. The abuse of language is a special concern to Orwell in many of his writings: here, in the novel, the ways in which language is distorted to form the banal, snappy, advertising slogans in the service of the 'money-god' draws particular venom. Edward Said castigates Orwell for representing Gordon Comstock, the anti-hero of the novel, for being 'indifferent to any sort of political solutions to the evils of the money world from which he is in flight' (Said 2000: 93-94). Yet, Orwell, through highlighting the crucial role of advertisements in the 'racket of capitalism', implicitly (and so all the more effectively) encourages action to counter the hyper-commercialism of society.

Moreover, while Orwell's influence on the formation of Cultural Studies as an academic disciple – with his remarkably original writings on such commonplace things as junk shops, cups of tea, sexy seaside postcards, boys' weeklies, cheap women's magazines, American crime novels and public houses – is now well-established, his crucial role in the creation of Media Studies is less well known

(Crook 2020). This paper has shown that in his many writings on advertisements he maintains a consistent political economy approach. Yet this is conveyed in always accessible and often witty prose free from jargon and befuddling theoretical abstraction. Today's academics have still a lot to learn from Orwell.

- The author would like to thank Professor Tim Crook for his comments on a draft of this paper. Responsibility for the final version, of course, rests with the author, alone.

REFERENCES

Bowker, Gordon (2003) *George Orwell*, London: Little, Brown

Crook, Tim (2020) Orwell and Media Studies, in email to author, 11 April

Dulley, Paul Richard (2015) *In Front of Your Nose: The Existentialism of George Orwell*. PhD thesis, University of Sussex. Available online at http://sro.sussex.ac.uk/id/eprint/56743/

Orwell, George (1970 [1928]) A farthing newspaper, Orwell, Sonia and Angus, Ian (eds) *The Collected Essays, Journalism and Letters of George Orwell, Vol. 1: An Age Like This, 1920-1940*, Harmondsworth, Middlesex: Penguin pp 34-37; *G. K.'s Weekly*, 29 December

Orwell, George (1976 [1936]) *Keep the Aspidistra Flying*, in Animal Farm and Other Novels, London: Secker and Warburg/Octopus pp 573-737

Orwell, George (1970 [1941a]) *The Lion and the Unicorn, The Collected Essays, Journalism and Letters of George Orwell, Vol. 2: My Country Right or Left 1940-1942*, Harmondsworth, Middlesex: Penguin pp 74-134; February 1941

Orwell, George (1970 [1941b]) London Letter to *Partisan Review*, Orwell, Sonia and Angus, Ian (eds) *The Collected Essays, Journalism and Letters of George Orwell, Vol. 2: My Country Right or Left, 1940-1942*, Harmondsworth, Middlesex: Penguin pp 137-149; 15 April

Orwell, George (1970 [1942]) London Letter to *Partisan Review*, Orwell, Sonia and Angus, Ian (eds) *The Collected Essays, Journalism and Letters of George Orwell, Vol. 2: My Country Right or Left, 1940-1942*, Harmondsworth, Middlesex: Penguin pp 265-272; November-December

Orwell, George (1970 [1943]) Review of *Beggar My Neighbour*, by Lionel Fielden, Orwell, Sonia and Angus, Ian (eds) *The Collected Essays, Journalism and Letters of George Orwell, Vol. 2: My Country Right or Left, 1940-1942*, Harmondsworth, Middlesex: Penguin pp 349-359; *Horizon*, September

Orwell, George (1998 [1944a]) As I Please, Davison, Peter (ed.) *Complete Works of George Orwell, Vol 16: I Have Tried to Tell The Truth, 1943-1944*, London: Secker and Warburg pp 145-148; *Tribune*, 7 April

Orwell, George (1998 [1944b]) As I Please, Davison, Peter (ed.) *Complete Works of George Orwell, Vol 16: I Have Tried to Tell The Truth, 1943-1944*, London: Secker and Warburg pp 103-104; *Tribune*, 25 February

Orwell, George (1998 [1944c]) As I Please, Davison, Peter (ed.) *Complete Works of George Orwell, Vol 16: I Have Tried to Tell The Truth, 1943-1944*, London: Secker and Warburg pp 251-253; *Tribune*, 9 June

Orwell, George (1998 [1944d]) As I Please, Davison, Peter (ed.) *Complete Works of George Orwell, Vol 16: I Have Tried to Tell The Truth, 1943-1944*, London: Secker and Warburg pp 463-465; *Tribune*, 17 November

Orwell, George (1998 [1946a]) As I Please, Davison, Peter (ed.) *Complete Works of George Orwell, Vol. 17: Smothered Under Journalism, 1946*, London: Secker and Warburg pp 471-472; *Tribune*, 8 November

RICHARD LANCE KEEBLE

Orwell, George (1998 [1946b]) As I Please, Davison, Peter (ed.) *Complete Works of George Orwell*, Vol. 17: *Smothered Under Journalism, 1946*, London: Secker and Warburg pp 497-500; *Tribune*, 22 November 1946

Orwell, George (2000 [1949]) *Nineteen Eighty-Four*, London: Penguin, with an introduction by Thomas Pynchon

Orwell, George (2010) *Diaries*, Davison, Peter (ed.) London: Penguin

Patai, Daphne (1984) *The Orwell Mystique: A Study in Male Ideology*, Amherst: University of Massachusetts Press

Said, Edward (2000) *Reflections on Exile: And Other Literary and Cultural Essays*, London: Granta

Topp, Sylvia (2020) *Eileen: The Making of George Orwell,* London: Unbound

Werbel, Amy Beth (2018) *Lust on Trial: Censorship and the Rise of American Obscenity in the Age of Anthony Comstock*, New York: Columbia University Press

Woloch, Alex (2016) *Or Orwell: Writing and Democratic Socialism*, Cambridge, Massachusetts: Harvard University Press

NOTE ON THE CONTRIBUTOR

Richard Lance Keeble's latest books are *Journalism Beyond Orwell* (Routledge, 2020) and *George Orwell, the Secret State and the Making of* Nineteen Eighty-Four (Abramis, 2020).

Eric and Alaric: Orwell and his Shadow

TIM CROOK

The 70th anniversary of the 1949 publication of Nineteen Eighty-Four *was attended by considerable panegyric and celebration of George Orwell and his novel. This paper, rather, analyses one of Orwell's most ardent critics – Alaric Jacob. Jacob was a fellow alumnus of St Cyprian's preparatory school in Eastbourne – which Orwell so despised if his posthumously published essay 'Such, Such Were the Joys' is to be believed. Jacob once said that if Orwell were Mozart, he would be his living Salieri: in other words, a relatively minor writer condemned to live in the shade of his more celebrated contemporary. More poignantly, Jacob and his first wife were on Orwell's notorious list of crypto-communists given to the government's secret propaganda unit, the Information Research Department, in 1949. The paper goes on to examine in detail Jacob's comments on Orwell's* Nineteen Eighty-Four *and his oeuvre in general – and concludes that 'Alaric Jacob and his views on Orwell and his works merit some consideration'.*

Keywords: *Nineteen Eighty-Four*, Alaric Jacob, Cold War, Soviet Union, communism, socialism

It could be argued that Alaric Jacob had an early career in authorship and journalism that Eric Arthur Blair would have died for. At the very least it would have attracted envy and yearning. The emotions may well have been especially poignant as Jacob had closely followed the George Orwell of 'Such, Such Were the Joys' to the Eastbourne preparatory school, St. Cyprian's, where Alaric recalled: 'There can be no doubt about the considerable impression he made there, for soon after I entered the school I was encouraged, as it were, to understudy him' (Jacob 1984: 63).

Alaric and Eric had so much in common and at the same time so little. They were both given discounted fees on account of their academic promise, they had been born into the Edwardian age with parents running Colonial India. They excelled at French, English and History. They both harboured ambitions to be successful writers. Their fluent spoken and written French, due in great part to the brilliant teaching of St Cyprian's headmistress Mrs Wilkes, enabled them to write and publish in the language. They both rebelled against the ideology and culture of British imperialism. They were both 'of the left', as it were.

Between 1933 and 1950 Eric wrote ten books including six novels and two collections of essays. Between 1930 and 1995 Alaric wrote eight books, one in French, and his *oeuvre* also included novels, one published when he was only 21. He had two plays produced professionally on the stage when he was only 17 and 18. Eric's alter ego George Orwell is undoubtedly one of the most successful and celebrated writers of the 20th century. Alaric only wrote as himself and is consigned to obscurity and oblivion in terms of cultural memory and significance.

He is not mentioned in the biographies by Crick (1980), Shelden (1991), Bowker (2003) and Meyers (2000). D. J. Taylor engages with him only in respect of how his representation of St Cyprian's, in his autobiography *Scenes From A Bourgeois Life*, supports Orwell's excoriating polemic on his schooldays (Taylor 2003: 33-34). In reality, their perception of Mr and Mrs Wilkes, the headmaster and headmistress of St Cyprian's who were nicknamed 'Flip' and 'Sambo', could not have been more diametrically opposed. Alaric was, perhaps, rather precocious in publishing his autobiography at the relatively early age of forty in 1949 in the same year and by Secker and Warburg, the same publisher of Orwell's *Nineteen Eighty-Four*.

John Newsinger is the only other Orwellian scholar to have referenced the wholly forgotten and apparently irrelevant Alaric Jacob in his 2018 study *Hope Lies in the Proles: George Orwell and the Left*. In a section sub-titled 'No slander is too gross', Newsinger analyses the absolute fury of the response to *Nineteen Eighty-Four* by British communists. He observes that the '…fury is still evident as late as 1984 when *Inside the Myth*, edited by Christopher Norris, was published by the CP publisher, Lawrence and Wishart' (Newsinger 2018: 139). Newsinger argues that 'Norris put together a truly disgraceful collection of essays with the sole intention of discrediting George Orwell' and they included 'Alaric Jacob, a fellow travelling journalist' who condemned *Nineteen Eighty-Four* as 'one of the most disgusting books ever written', a book that put the works of the Marquis de Sade in the shade, it was so full of 'fear, hatred, lies and self-disgust' (ibid).

SHARING ORWELL'S 'JOYS' BUT NOT HIS FEARS

It could be argued that Alaric Jacob's essay in the Lawrence and Wishart volume is not so much disgraceful as more of a fascinating evaluation of Orwell by a writer from the same class and background. Jacob never wavered in his own faith in communism and came to loathe what he saw as dangerous flaws and consequences flowing from the older St Cyprian alumnus's democratic socialism. It may be somewhat ironic that Alaric's rage at Eric produced some of his best writing. He certainly approached the task with some wit and self-reflexivity:

> His dominant aim, as he said, was 'to make political writing into an art'. In this, after years of struggling to purify his style, he ultimately succeeded. But just as it is possible to admire the art of Machiavelli while refusing to enter the political blind alley into which the reader is artfully directed, so one may admire the clarity and simplicity of Orwell's style and yet stand aghast before some of the tortuous conclusions that he reaches. The truth is that Orwell lacks political judgment to a quite astonishing degree. … I shall not make myself popular among those latter-day admirers who have described Orwell as 'almost a saint' by venturing to compare my life style with his but, after all, their Mozart is secure upon his pedestal; Salieri still lives though no one is obliged to take him seriously (Jacob 1984: 62 and 72).

The chapter becomes a remarkable deconstruction and mocking of Jacob's own failures and lost dreams in the midst of his attack on the literary super-star who would haunt him. His inability to match Orwell's ability in Latin and Geek meant Alaric went on to King's School, Canterbury, without winning a place there as a King's Scholar (ibid: 63). Orwell, of course, gained scholarships to both Wellington and Eton. But when comparing their respective lives, Jacob manages at the same time to elevate his family and personal achievements above those of Orwell. Jacob certainly believed he had the better absent father: 'Orwell's father had married an attractive woman much younger than himself, as my father had done, but he had eked out a dull existence in minor postings. He had no legacy of scholarship or adventure to pass on to his son' (ibid: 64). During the Great War, Orwell's father was a mere 60-year-old lieutenant looking after horses in the South of France. In contrast Jacob's father commanded 'an army corps on the Western Front' and gave him envelopes for his stamp collection addressed to 'Major-General le Grand Jacob CB CMG CIE CBE DSO' and on his first, and last, visit to the school wore a Colonel's uniform adorned with the decorations of Star of India and French Legion of Honour (ibid: 66).

Jacob and Blair both have older women mentors for their writing careers – the latter starting much later than the former. Blair's family friend, Ruth Pitter (who would go on to win the Queen's Prize for Poetry) found her protégé's early writings inept and laughable and 'did not believe that he had it in him to make a living as an author' (ibid: 73). By contrast, Jacob is sponsored by Margot Asquith from the age of 19 who advises: 'I am sorry you have done a novel so young' after Methuen publish his first novel *Seventeen* when he

TIM CROOK

is only twenty-one (ibid: 74). While Blair is 'in truth a very slow developer. Even after his Burmese days and his apprenticeship in Paris, some of the English friends who tried to encourage his free-lance writing doubted his capacity to succeed' (ibid: 73), Jacob apprentices in journalism on a newspaper in Plymouth and is appointed diplomatic correspondent for Reuters at the age of majority. He goes on to represent that international news agency in Washington D.C. soon afterwards.

Jacob has a glamorous and dramatic career as foreign correspondent. He witnesses first-hand so much more history of the century in which he lives compared to the author of *Animal Farm* and *Nineteen Eighty-Four*. Like Orwell, he experiences the London blitz of 1940, but in 1941 is sent by Reuters to cover the fighting in North Africa, southern Russia and Burma. His obituarist in the *Independent*, Richard Jones says:

> This period inspired his book *A Traveller's War* (1944). By the time it was published, he was already back in Russia, now representing the *Daily Express*. He had sailed to Russia in an Arctic convoy accompanied by his wife, Iris Morley (they had married in 1933), who represented the *Observer* and the *Yorkshire Post*. Iris Morley was a communist whose ideas strongly influenced Jacob. He later said that his time in Russia was one of the great formative experiences of his life. Jacob was attached to the Red Army from Stalingrad to the fall of Berlin (Jones 1995).

Jacob has contacts in the highest echelons of political life in Washington and Moscow. After the Second World War, he has a career in the BBC lasting 24 years, finally retiring in 1972 as a senior editor at the BBC's World Service in Bush House 'where his fair-mindedness, flair and coolness under pressure were greatly appreciated' (ibid). Orwell lasted only two years at the BBC. It is from this perspective that Jacob can write in 1984:

> Notwithstanding his rebellious beginnings in Burma, the days of Bohemian struggle in Paris and his gallant expedition to Spain, he was not a widely travelled man. Russia and America were unknown to him. He was at heart an Edwardian Little Englander, basically uninterested in the life-styles of other peoples, so it is hardly surprising that his politics were often naïve. His lifelong, unrequited love affair with the English working class also contributed to a lack of balance as did his six wretched, friendless years at St Cyprian's School (Jacob 1984: 63).

Jacob cannot resist mixing his criticism with much put-down and jealous angst. It may be because the person he was writing about has faced a lifetime of wretched health with a depressive temperament, has hated sports and enjoyed success and literary immortality while he himself would fail despite having 'scarcely known a day's illness ... enjoyed being in the first eleven at cricket and in the shooting eight' (ibid: 72).

Jacob believes truth should have been on his side for 'The truth as I saw it was that the Wilkes family [who ran St Cyprian's] for all their faults, were not monsters and that the education they offered was, within the cramped ethos of that time, admirable' (ibid). In *Scenes From A Bourgeois Life,* Jacob calls the school St. Saviour's and the Wilkes are given the pseudonym Arbuthnot:

> The school was administered with great shrewdness and efficiency by the headmaster's wife, a fat and untidy Scotswoman who loved to *épater les bourgeois* by the freedom of her language which, so thought Messieurs les Nouveaux Riches, gave a racy, aristocratic air to all that she undertook. She had a good heart and used the swollen profits she obtained from the parvenus to subsidise the careers of the new poor (Jacob 1949: 50).

SPAIN AND THE SOVIET UNION – CONTRASTING VIEWPOINTS

Jacob continues to allege, quite vituperatively, that Orwell lacks balance in his understanding and writing about the Spanish Civil War and the Soviet Union in *Homage To Catalonia, Animal Farm* and *Nineteen Eighty-Four*. The problem for Alaric is that Eric has actually been in Spain and witnessed the agony, betrayal and defeat. He writes from visceral personal experience. As Jacob later concedes:

> At the time I used to feel guilty about holding a well-paid job as Reuters' correspondent in Washington while Orwell was risking his life in the front line (he nearly lost it when he was shot through the neck by a sniper), and I used to have arguments with American friends as to whether I ought not to resign and join the International Brigade. Most of them urged me to wait for the much bigger war we were certain was coming (Jacob 1984: 77).

It seems Jacob and Orwell never met. Certainly, having read *Homage to Catalonia*, Jacob says there are many questions he would have liked to put to him for discussion because he has been astonished that anyone 'so experienced and intelligent' could have misread the situation so completely:

> The gist of his argument was that the Spanish Republic had been betrayed not by Britain, France or the United States, who by refusing all aid were ensuring Franco's victory, but by Russia – the only country which was in fact sending help (ibid).

TIM CROOK

Jacob goes on to denounce a lack of political balance in *Animal Farm* which he describes as unstable because the book has been 'misused for political purposes in a manner which Orwell might have foreseen had his own political antennae been more sensitive than they were' (ibid: 79). Jacob debunks the claim that *Nineteen Eighty-Four* is an attack on Fascism and Nazism because: 'We know that neither Hitler nor Mussolini abolished the capitalist system; on the contrary, private wealth continued to accumulate' (ibid: 81). He continues:

> Ingsoc has triumphed, the old system of private enterprise has gone for ever. Big Brother rules over a squalid, poverty-stricken society in which the Party bosses retain some semblance of what had once been a good life. Ingsoc is, in fact, no more than a projection of the kind of regime which extreme anti-Communists have always envisaged as existing in the USSR since 1917 and which anyone who has lived in that country, as I have done, knows to be a travesty of the truth. Despite all the stupidities, errors and crimes that have been committed in the name of Marx, it is absurd to suggest that the millions who live in the Communist world are universally downtrodden and depressed. Aspiration, ambition, love and the pursuit of happiness are as common in Moscow as they are in Manchester (ibid: 81-82).

It would seem that Jacob sees the betrayal of socialism as the key cultural detonator in *Nineteen Eighty-Four*:

> To write a book like *Nineteen Eighty-Four* is to present a gift of inestimable value to those who hate socialism and who would wish, as Churchill once did, to 'strangle it at birth'. In the thirty years and more since Orwell died several generations have been indoctrinated with the idea that socialism leads inexorably to the horrors described in that book. This is a lie but it is widely believed, and the man who launched it is the same wretched little boy who was so unhappy at St Cyprian's School (ibid: 82).

JACOB'S CRITICISM – BARBED WIRE WRAPPED AROUND HIS LIGHTWEIGHT (SIZE 8) SHOES

It could be argued that any authority in Jacob's analysis is undermined by his nasty and excoriating tone. The carefully crafted turn of phrase has a tendency to descend into invective. The quotation in full which impells Newsinger to condemn the Norris volume *Inside The Myth* as disgraceful is an example:

> For me *Nineteen Eighty-Four* is one of the most disgusting books ever written – a book smelling of fear, hatred, lies and self-disgust by comparison with which the works of the Marquis de Sade are no more than the bad dreams of a sick mind. Only a very sick man could have written it, and six months after it appeared Orwell was dead (ibid: 81).

This is a passage Orwell's character Squealer in *Animal Farm* would have been proud of. It was preceded with insouciant and sarcastic, public school style mockery: 'Not for anything would I have been in Orwell's shoes nor he, of course, in mine. He was a heavyweight (size 12 in boots); I a lightweight (size 8 shoes)' (ibid).

Jacob's problem may well have been that he projects his own lack of balance and propensity for exaggeration on to Orwell. And this may well have been combined with very good reasons for personal enmity. He can certainly be categorised as one of the Soviet Union's useful idiots. He does not have the perspective and experience of reporting iconoclastically in the Soviet Union during the 1930s like Gareth Richard Vaughan Jones and Malcolm Muggeridge. His contact with the Russians is during the heroic struggle for survival following Hitler's 1941 invasion in Operation Barbarossa. His romantic view of Marxism in terms of the Soviet communist context as creatively extoled in his 1962 novel *Two Ways In The World* could be seen as naïve and inappropriate as anything written by his bête noir author of *Nineteen Eighty-Four*.

It is certainly swimming against the tide to run the political prose argument 'despite the follies and errors of the regime, despite the horrible crimes committed in the name of communism, the society that he sees the Russians building is basically a just one. Compared with it, life at home in England seems to him a stagnant, shabby affair' (Jacob 1962: 1). Yet the millions experiencing life in the Gulag would not have been able to appreciate the spirit of the 'maverick in the herd' central character of Jacob's unsuccessful and utterly forgotten novel.

There is another reason for Alaric to hate Eric. He and his first wife are included in the notorious list of people with pro-communist leanings prepared in March 1949 by George Orwell for his friend Celia Kirwan at the Information Research Department, a propaganda unit set up at the Foreign Office by the Labour government. Alaric certainly writes publicly about being 'trapped in the bosom of MI5 at the BBC' (Jacob 1985).

Jacob joins the BBC in August 1948 at the monitoring service in Caversham, but in February 1951 he is 'suddenly refused establishment rights, which meant he would receive no pension' (ibid). He complains unsuccessfully to his second cousin, Sir Ian Jacob, who was prominent in the BBC and later became the organisation's director general.

Some have attributed Jacob's problems to the fact that his name was on Orwell's list. He had certainly been 'colleged' by the internal BBC system of MI5 vetting and surveillance. The red Christmas Tree symbol, indicating suspicious political views, would have been on his staff file.

PAPER

But it is also a fact that his establishment and pension rights were restored shortly after his wife Iris Morley – the Communist Party member and Marxist historian – died in 1953. Timothy Garton Ash argues that 'A two-year loss of BBC "establishment rights" is hardly *Darkness at Noon* or a session with the rats in Room 101. Anyway, there is thus far no evidence that Orwell's list had anything at all to do with the temporary blacklisting of Alaric Jacob 20 months later' (Garton Ash 2003).

Much has been written about Orwell's list, particularly by the main biographers (Shelden 1991: 467-469; Meyers 2000: 296; Taylor 2003: 408-409; Bowker 2003: 428-430). Richard Lance Keeble's interview with Orwell's friend and editor of the *Observer*, David Astor, offers an opinion about why he would have drawn it up and provided the information to a friend working in the Foreign Office's organisation set up to counter Soviet propaganda during the Cold War:

> These people were working for the British government while being active sympathisers or 'fellow travellers' with the Soviet Union. The government would not have wanted to employ them if this affiliation had been known to them. I don't think Orwell was doing anything wrong in exposing them (Keeble 2020: 42).

THE CRITICAL APPROACH TO ORWELL'S POLITICAL WRITING

It would be wrong to say that the 70-year commemoration of *Nineteen Eight-Four* publication has been devoid of any criticism. D. J Taylor, in *On* Nineteen Eight-Four*: A Biography*, deals with the Raymond Williams charge that 'As a Marxist, he can never quite forgive Orwell for taking his model from Soviet Communism, or for creating – however unthinkingly – a propaganda tool that could be used by the parties of the Right' (Taylor 2019: 144). Dorian Lynskey, in *The Ministry of Truth: A Biography of George Orwell's* 1984, highlights the problems and consequences of the novel's afterlife:

> *The Spectator's* Paul Johnson observed that this 'ideological overkill' could only result in a tie: 'Since everyone, Left, Right and Centre, can and does hijack the wretched man for every conceivable political purpose, the net result is almost exactly nil.' Still, nobody considered the possibility that the ranks of those attempting to appropriate Orwell would include Russian propagandists (Lynskey 2019: 245).

Moreover, critics in the 1984 volume include the late Stuart Hall, then Professor of Sociology at the Open University who, when exploring the subject of 'Conjuring Leviathan: Orwell on the State', argues that the tendency to keep asking the question 'Was Orwell right?' is a hopeless approach, 'since he was so often right *and* wrong, sometimes in succession, more often in the same moment.

Despite the claims on moral clarity and political honesty which his style makes for him, his political writing was shot through with ambiguities and, in the final analysis, deeply contradictory' (Hall 1984: 217-218). Beatrix Campbell, then a journalist at *City Limits*, author of *Wigan Pier Revisited* and later contributor to *Marxism Today* and the *New Statesman*, advances one of the first feminist critiques in her chapter, 'Orwell – Paterfamilias or Big Brother'.

Orwell may even have had some fun with Antony Easthope, teacher of English and Cultural Studies at Manchester Polytechnic who in 'Fact and fantasy in *Nineteen Eighty-Four*', argues:

> By continually enforcing an either/or – either the absolute immobility of the real represented transparently in language, or the abyss of words which are only words – the novel tends to negate what it intended. Instead of confirming the truth of the text it subverts it. Surely the conscientious use of a realist's narrative means us to overlook the means of representation in favour of what is represented, to accede to the prose style as something weightless and without origin? And what happens? Continuous insistence on writing pushes into the foreground the text's own discourse, making us ask what it is and where it comes from. If it originates in the present, how can it have access to this narrative from 1984? (Easthope 1984: 273-274)

It is classic piece of Cultural Studies gobbledygook – an example of academic and political writing which Orwell complained about in his essay 'Politics and the English Language', of 1946.

PUTTING THE GENIE BACK IN THE BOTTLE

Alaric Jacob's criticism of Orwell for failing to consider adequately *Nineteen Eighty-Four's* impact on socialism is confirmed by the clumsiness and desperation of Orwell's post-publication attempt to explain and correct. Significantly, he put out a media release complaining that:

> My recent novel is NOT intended as an attack on Socialism or on the British Labour Party (of which I am a supporter) but as a show-up of the perversions to which a centralised economy is liable and which have already been partly realised in Communism and Fascism. I do not believe that the kind of society I describe necessarily will arrive, but I believe (allowing of course for the fact that the book is a satire) that something resembling it could arrive (Davison 1998: 135).

Raymond Williams is clear that Orwell identifies 'oligarchical collectivism' directly with the Soviet system; not capitalism. He remains a democratic socialist and gives 'most of his political energies to the defence of civil liberties over a wide front':

TIM CROOK

But in his deepest vision of what was to come, he had at once actualized a general nightmare and then, in the political currents of the time, narrowed its reference until the nightmare itself became one of its own shaping elements (Williams 1971: 68).

The charge from the left remains. As Williams complains: 'What in Orwell broke down in terror became a comfortable and persistent world view (in an older generation even lasting beyond Vietnam)' (ibid: 93-94). Williams argues that Orwell's political prophecy and speculation about the future proves to be problematical because he fails to foresee how 'affluent and militarist capitalism, or a world of international corporations' would 'function, internally and externally, very much like his projected Party' (ibid: 77).

Orwell should have known that *Nineteen Eighty-Four* would be seen as an attack on the British Labour Party and socialism:

> Ingsoc, it might then be said, is no more English Socialism than Minitrue is the Ministry of Truth. But the identification was in effect made, and has been profoundly damaging. Not in what it says about Soviet society … but in what it implied generally about socialism and a centralized economy. … By assigning all modern forms of repression and authoritarian control to a single political tendency, he not only misrepresented it, but cut short the kind of analysis that would recognize these inhuman and destructive forces wherever they appeared, under whatever names, and masked by whatever ideology (ibid: 76-77).

HOW ORWELL PROVOKED THE LEFT'S REVENGE ON HIS LEGACY

Alaric Jacob's denunciation of Orwell's political writing is intemperate, polemical and angry – just as Orwell's could be. When he says all tobacconists are fascists, that could be funny and fine if you are not a tobacconist. In *The Road To Wigan* Pier, he writes:

> We have reached a stage when the very word 'Socialism' calls up, on the one hand, a picture of aeroplanes, tractors and huge glittering factories of glass and concrete; on the other, a picture of vegetarians with wilting beards, of Bolshevik commissars (half gangster, half gramophone), of earnest ladies in sandals, shock-headed Marxists chewing polysyllables, escaped Quakers, birth-control fanatics and Labour Party backstairs-crawlers. Socialism, at least in this island, does not smell any longer of revolution and the overthrow of tyrants, it smells of crankishness, machine-worship and the stupid cult of Russia (Orwell 1937: 248).

Such remarks could not be calculated to cause more offence. Throughout his essay writing he has a regular line on 'pansies' – the pejorative insult for homosexuals. His hero H. G. Wells was never the same again after Orwell juxtaposed him with Hitler in the title of a critical essay about his political legitimacy. Jacob was certainly dishing out as much as Orwell gave.

SOME CONCLUDING THOUGHTS

Alaric Jacob and his views on Orwell and his works merit some consideration. In the bigger picture he makes an important contribution to fostering an understanding and appreciation of the suffering and struggle of the Russian people during the terrible war in the East, which most likely decided the outcome of the Second World War. But journalistically and to a lesser extent through his fiction and non-fiction, Jacob has lost the argument about the threat to human rights, freedom and liberty posed by Soviet totalitarian communism. Orwell, had he lived as long as his shadow, may well have appreciated engaging in the argument.

It is interesting to note that in the same year Secker and Warburg brings out *Nineteen Eighty-Four* with an initial print-run of 25,000, it also publishes Jacob's autobiographical *Scenes From A Bourgeois Life* and this book's first print-run never exceeds 3,000. As Jacob stresses: 'The irony of our respective situations seemed to me to have been underwritten by the Gods' (Jacob 1984: 81). *Nineteen Eighty-Four* would be a 'veritable shower of gold' descending 'upon Orwell from vast sales in America and from translation rights all over the world; so much so that he had to be turned into a limited company to safeguard the future of his estate' (ibid).

The envy is palpable. At the end of his essay, Jacob comments: 'Unable to cherish his memory, yet unable to get him out of my mind, I have written a book about Orwell and his contemporaries which, like "Such, Such Were the Joys", will probably not be published until all of us are dead' (ibid: 83-84). Indeed, Orwell's Salieri remains a largely unknown figure – even 25 years after his passing.

REFERENCES

Bowker, Gordon (2003) *George Orwell*, London: Little, Brown

Campbell, Beatrix (1984) Orwell – Paterfamilias or Big Brother? Norris, Christopher (ed.) *Inside the Myth: Orwell: Views from the Left*, London: Lawrence and Wishart pp 126-138

Crick, Bernard (1980) *George Orwell: A Life*, Harmondsworth, Middlesex: Penguin

Davison, Peter (ed.) (1998) *The Complete Works of George Orwell, Vol. XX, Our Job is to Make Life Worth Living, 1949-1950*, London: Secker and Warburg

Easthope, Antony (1984) Fact and fantasy in *Nineteen Eighty-Four*, Norris, Christopher (ed.) *Inside the Myth: Orwell: Views from the Left*, London: Lawrence and Wishart pp 263-285

Garton Gash, Timothy (2003) Love, death and treachery, *Guardian*, 21 June

TIM CROOK

Hall, Stuart (1984) Conjuring Leviathan: Orwell on the state, Norris, Christopher (ed.) *Inside the Myth: Orwell: Views from the Left*, London: Lawrence and Wishart pp 217-241

Jacob, Alaric (1930) *Seventeen: A Novel Of School Life*, London: Methuen & Co. Ltd

Jacob, Alaric (1944) *A Traveller's War: A Journey to the Wars in Africa, India and Russia*, London: Collins

Jacob, Alaric (1946) *A Window in Moscow 1944-45*, London: Collins

Jacob, Alaric (1949) *Scenes From A Bourgeois Life: The Autobiography of Alaric Jacob*, London: Secker and Warburg

Jacob, Alaric (1962) *Two Ways in the World*, London: Eyre and Spottiswoode

Jacob, Alaric (1969) *A Russian Journey from Suzdal to Samarkand*, New York: Hill and Wang

Jacob, Alaric (1971) *Eminent Nonentities*, London: The Galahad Press

Jacob, Alaric (1984) Sharing Orwell's 'joys' – but not his fears, Norris, Christopher (ed.) (1984) *Inside the Myth: Orwell: Views from the Left*, London: Lawrence and Wishart pp 62-84

Jacob, Alaric (1985) How I got padlocked by MI5's in Auntie's bosom, *The Observer*, 25 August

Jones, Richard (1995) Obituary: Alaric Jacob, *Independent*, 8 February. Available online at https://www.independent.co.uk/news/people/alaric-jacob-1572017.html, accessed on 23 September 2020

Keeble, Richard Lance (2020) *George Orwell, The Secret State And The Making Of Nineteen Eighty Four*, Bury St Edmunds: Abramis

Lynskey, Dorian (2019) *The Ministry of Truth: A Biography of George Orwell's 1984*, London: Picador

Meyers, Jeffrey (2000) *Orwell: Wintry Conscience of a Generation*, New York and London: W. W. Norton and Company Ltd

Newsinger, John (2018) *Hope Lies In The Proles: George Orwell and the Left*, London: Pluto Press

Norris, Christopher (ed.) (1984) *Inside the Myth: Orwell: Views from the Left*, London: Lawrence and Wishart

Orwell, George (1937) *The Road To Wigan Pier*, London: Victor Gollancz Ltd

Shelden, Michael (1991) *Orwell: The Authorised Biography*, London: William Heinemann

Taylor, D. J. (2003) *Orwell: The Life*, London: Chatto and Windus

Taylor, D. J. (2019) *On Nineteen Eighty-Four: A Biography*, New York: Abrams Press

Williams, Raymond (1971) *Orwell*, London: Fontana/Collins

Williams, Raymond (ed.) (1974) *George Orwell: A Collection of Critical Essays*, New Jersey: Prentice Hall

NOTE ON THE CONTRIBUTOR

Tim Crook is Emeritus Professor at Goldsmiths, University of London. President of the Chartered Institute of Journalists and longstanding author, journalist and academic, he is also joint editor of *George Orwell Studies* and is currently completing a monograph for Ashgate on 'Orwell on the Radio'.

ARTICLE

Each Herself – Fact, Fiction and Female Identity

Ann Kronbergs, the author of a forthcoming collection of short stories, *Each Herself*, about the women in George Orwell's life, explains how she came to write these stories, how she blended fact and fiction and how she was inspired by a range of sources and angles on these women's lives.

WHY THE SHORT STORY FORM?

An unreliable eyewitness account of a sighting of Eric Blair in the 1920s gave me the germ of an idea, twenty years before I wrote it, for the short story 'No Going Back'. The following account appeared in 1993, in a local newsletter in Church Stretton, Shropshire, written by an elderly local cricketer reminiscing about his days as a member of the local cricket club in the 1920s:

> I still have memories of a tall, saturnine character who turned out regularly each summer for Birtley [a village close by] whilst staying with his friend … at Ticklerton. To us he was chiefly notable for his habit of always fielding on the boundary to facilitate his non-stop production and consumption of hand-rolled 'fags'; we knew him simply as Eric Blair and it was not until 1984 that his better known identity as George Orwell registered, at least with me.

This reminiscence led me to make a vain attempt to trace Eric Blair's cricketing history in Birtley, but that trail soon went dead. There were no extant records of any local village cricket clubs from that time and, in any case, as Bernard Crick's biography of George Orwell reveals (1980), there were very few possible dates in that decade when Eric Blair may have been in Shropshire, playing cricket or otherwise. In other words, this eye-witness account was a false memory, a fusion of fact and fiction. As historical fact it was unreliable; as suggestive fiction, however, it opened up for me at that time a tiny keyhole view of Eric Blair's association with the Buddicom family of Ticklerton Court.

Spool forward to A. L. Kennedy's Orwell Memorial Lecture, *Orwell with Women* (2017). In her talk, the writer adopted a snapshot approach to her discussion of Orwell's relationships with women, exploring what we may intuit from a selection of moments in time,

ANN KRONBERGS

whether caught on camera or in letter form. Take, for example, Orwell on the beach in Southwold with Eleanor Jaques in 1932, Orwell and his first wife Eileen O'Shaughnessy with a POUM attachment in Spain in 1937, or Orwell in a letter to Brenda Salkeld in 1934. In essence, A. L. Kennedy's snapshots were oral tales, glimpsing the female perspective for moments in Orwell's packed life. These tales were pithy, rooted in the detail of a particular time and place, and for me they showed how the short-story form might be used to decentre Orwell from his own story and allow the women in his life to be foregrounded.

Whilst A. L. Kennedy's oral tales covered Orwell's life in a patchy and unresolved way, they opened up to me the possibility of creating a short-story collection that could be like an album in which 'snapshot' narratives reveal the lives and experiences of Orwell's women, including many spaces and chronological gaps, but nevertheless building a sense of completeness overall. The eventual collection follows a linear chronology from 1927 through to 1950, glimpsing the lives of particular women close to Orwell in those years.

Throughout this writing endeavour the National Writing Centre in Norwich has been a source of mentoring support and, in 2019, I also attended a University of Cambridge Short Story Festival to gather ideas from contemporary writers and editors. The Orwell Society has provided scope for added enrichment with visits to actual places where Orwell lived and worked, including Booklovers' Corner, in Hampstead, the Stores and St Mary's Church, in Wallington, Hertfordshire, and, most impressively of all, Barnhill on the remote Scottish island of Jura, where Orwell spent his final years composing *Nineteen Eighty-Four*. In addition, the Orwell Archive at UCL has offered the opportunity to consult a wealth of original papers, and both the archives of the Southwold Museum, Suffolk, and the on-line Shropshire County Council archive have also proved formative for this project.

FACT AND FICTION IN THE STORIES THEMSELVES

Clearly each of the individual women associated with Orwell has her separate history. How to determine and make use of accurate chronological detail and historical fact as a source for the short stories has been the biggest challenge. The more high-profile women, such as Eileen or his second wife, Sonia Brownell, have received significant attention from biographers in recent years; we also have their letters and other documents to draw on. This material has been formative in determining how to dramatise each of these women at crucial moments in time and place. The less high-profile women, such as Orwell's sister Avril or his Aunt Nellie, have presented a greater research challenge because the historical record is obscure at times. Despite this, it has been possible to construct their timelines and to use available documentary evidence as source material for their stories.

The first story of the collection, 'No Going Back', opens in Southwold in 1927. As source material for the brief representation of Avril Blair and the world of her Copper Kettle Tea Room I used the 1920s oral accounts of Southwold inhabitants in *Remembering Orwell*, edited by Stephen Wadhams (1984). For Eric Blair's dilemma when he returned from Burma, I consulted the biographies of both Bernard Crick (1980) and D. J. Taylor (2004 [2003]). Jacintha Buddicom's memoir *Eric & Us* (2006 [1974]). And my own familiarity with the local area provided background for the representation of Ticklerton Court and the portrayal of Aunt Lilian Hayward. The resulting short story hinges on Eric's personal crisis at the outset of his writing career, his desire to reclaim a footing in the lost world of Ticklerton Court and his need to make telephone contact with Jacintha. During the writing of this story new information about Jacintha's exact location in London at this time, with her illegitimate baby daughter, came to light, enabling the ending of the story to have a more poignant twist.

The next story, 'Poissons d'Avril', focuses on Orwell's Aunt Nellie and offers snapshots of her life between 1928 and 1936. The particular personal history of this remarkable woman has largely remained hidden from biographers, who have tended to marginalise her role and influence on her nephew, with the exception of Gordon Bowker, who noted that Nellie 'would have more influence on his literary and political development than any other member of his family' (Bowker 2003: 12). Recently, due to the research of Darcy Moore (2020), Nellie Limouzin has emerged from the shadows. Moore has uncovered the extent of her suffragette activism, leading to her arrest and imprisonment. He has also produced evidence of her theatrical career in London and her growing politicisation, which eventually led her to espouse the Esperantist cause and to settle in Paris where she lived with a fellow activist, Eugène Adam or 'Lanti'. Moore shows the pivotal role of this pair as political mentors for the penniless Eric Blair in Paris in 1928 and makes a clear case for the practical and literary assistance provided by Nellie to her nephew at the outset of his writing career. In representing her in the short story 'Poissons d'Avril' I used three locations: her flats in London and Paris, and the Stores in Wallington. The story highlights Nellie's selfless devotion to Eric's career as a writer, her relationship with Lanti and the rise and fall in her circumstances by the mid-thirties.

The third story of the collection, 'Unfinished Letter', focuses on Eileen Blair in the last few weeks of her life, between February and March 1945, when Orwell was away in France and Germany working as a foreign correspondent for the *Observer*. This was when she and their adopted son, Richard, stayed with her sister-in-law Gwen O'Shaughnessy in the house called Greystone near

Newcastle-upon-Tyne. A photograph of the house (in Sylvia Topp's biography, of 2020) and Eileen's own letters to Orwell from this time, give the context. With the benefit of hindsight, we can see all too clearly how the sands of time were running out for Eileen, though neither she nor Orwell realised this. It's evident how crucial the medical advice and treatment were to the final tragic outcome. So I present her gradually deteriorating physical condition through a series of scenes with Gwen at Greystone, in the consulting rooms of her gynaecologist near Newcastle, and finally in the hospital where she had her fatal operation.

Sonia Brownell presents the trickiest challenge among Orwell's women as a subject for a short story. As Jeffrey Meyers states (2020):

> … everyone I interviewed for my biography thought she married the moribund Orwell for his literary fame and great wealth, which he could not spend.

Although Hilary Spurling attempted to set the record straight with her more sympathetic portrayal in *The Girl From the Fiction Department* (2002), the idea of Sonia the gold-digger – promoted largely by men – has tended to triumph over Spurling's view of the golden-hearted Sonia. In 'The Cemetery of Lost Love', I try to tread carefully, representing the changes in her personal and working life during the course of 1949. This was the year in which she moved from being a sub-editor on Cyril Connolly's *Horizon* magazine to become the wife of George Orwell, world-famous author of the recent literary phenomenon *Nineteen Eighty-Four*. In this story I try to track Sonia's feelings and motivations across the year which changed her life and led to the end of Orwell's.

The first and last stories provide a framing structure for the collection, dramatising the beginning and end of Orwell's writing life. 'Closing Time', which rounds off the collection, is mostly set in Christ Church, Albany Street, and draws on the accounts of Orwell's funeral on 26 January 1950 given by Malcolm Muggeridge and on D. J. Taylor's description of the event in the first chapter of his biography (2004 [2003]). The church had been the poet Christina Rossetti's place of worship and her brother, Dante Gabriel Rossetti, designed the stained-glass panel in one of the east-facing windows. This particular setting, along with the music of the hymns and the words of the readings, offers a curiously fitting backdrop to the finale of the story with a focus on the viewpoints of the three female characters: Avril, Eileen and Jacintha.

CONCLUSION

In her Reith lecture, Hilary Mantel (2017) argues that by choosing historical fiction, readers are 'actively requesting a subjective interpretation of the evidence'. The writer's task, as she sees it, is 'to recreate the texture of lived experience: to activate the senses, and to deepen the reader's engagement through feeling'. Whilst I have used the historical record to inform how I represent each of the women in this short-story collection, my main purpose in each narrative has been to dramatise moments in their experience, to show their reality within the overarching story of George Orwell's own life, but without allowing them to be overshadowed by this literary giant. For the title of this collection, *Each Herself – Stories of Women in the Life of George Orwell*, I have taken a phrase from Eileen Blair's poem *End of the Century, 1984* (see Topp 2020: 84-85) to emphasise the importance of female identity at the heart of the stories.

ACKNOWLEDGEMENT

I am obliged to Dione Venables for sharing further information about the exact whereabouts of Jacintha in the autumn of 1927 when Eric Blair attempted to make telephone contact with her in London.

REFERENCES

Bowker, Gordon (2009 [2003]) *George Orwell*, London: Abacus

Buddicom, Jacintha (2006 [1974]) *Eric & Us,* Chichester: Finlay Publisher

Crick, Bernard (1980) *George Orwell: A Life*: Harmondsworth, Middlesex: Penguin

Kennedy, A. L. (2017) The Orwell Memorial Lecture: *Orwell with Women*. Available online at https://www.orwellfoundation.com/the-orwell-foundation/programmes/the-orwell-lecture-2/#:~:text=The%20Orwell%20Lecture%202017%3A%20A.%20L.&text=Kennedy%20said%3A%20%E2%80%9CDeeply%20associated%20with,centre%20of%20his%20imaginative%20life.

Mantel, Hilary (2017) The BBC Reith Lecture. Available online at https://www.bbc.co.uk/programmes/b08tcbrp

Meyers, Jeffrey (2020) Memoirs of Orwell: The quest for truth, *George Orwell Studies*, Vol. 4, No. 1 pp 85-97

Moore, Darcy (2020) Orwell's Aunt Nellie, *George Orwell Studies*, Vol. 4, No. 2 pp 30-44

Muggeridge, Malcolm (1971) A knight of the woeful countenance, Gross, Miriam (ed.) *The World of George Orwell*, London: Weidenfeld & Nicolson pp 165-175

Orwell, George (2010) *A Life in Letters*, Davison, Peter (ed.) London: Penguin

Spurling, Hilary (2002) *The Girl from The Fiction Department: A Portrait of Sonia Orwell*, London: Hamish Hamilton

Taylor, D. J. (2004 [2003]) *Orwell: The Life,* London: Vintage

Topp, Sylvia (2020) *Eileen – The Making of George Orwell*, London: Unbound

Wadhams, Stephen (1984) *Remembering Orwell*, Harmondsworth: Middlesex: Penguin

ANN KRONBERGS

NOTE ON THE CONTRIBUTOR

Ann Kronbergs writes fiction, essays, feature articles and reviews and is an experienced teacher and lecturer. Her publications include work on Shakespeare in performance and Orwell. She is a trustee of The Orwell Society. She has published a novel *Diamond Edelweiss* (2020). See www.cabottepress.co.uk.

ARTICLE

The Hôpital Cochin and the Extraordinary Life (And Death) of Marthe Hanau

George Orwell, in his article 'How the Poor Die', describes an appalling ward in Hôpital X in Paris's 15th arrondissement where he spent several days – from 7 March until 22 March – in 1929 following a bad attack of influenza. It was actually the Hôpital Cochin in the 14th arrondissement. In the article, Orwell states that a 'year or two later the celebrated swindler Madame Hanau, who was ill while on remand, was taken to the Hôpital X and after a few days of it she managed to elude her guards, took a taxi and drove back to the prison, explaining that she was more comfortable there' (Orwell 1970 [1946]: 264). Here, John P. Lethbridge looks at the history of Hôpital Cochin. He then examines in more detail Marthe Hanau's extraordinary life and describes the facts behind Orwell's brief reference to her.

THE HÔPITAL COCHIN

The Hôpital Cochin was founded by Jean-Denis Cochin (1726-1783), the Roman Catholic parish priest of the Parish of St Jacques de Haut Pas, Paris, as a hospice for the poor in 1780 (Herbermann 1913). Initially run by the Sisters of Charity, i.e. Catholic nuns, it was called the Hôpital Saint-Jacques, but in 1801 the General Council of the Paris Hospitals renamed it after its founder. Until Orwell arrived there its most famous patient was the mathematician Évariste Galois. Leopold Infeld's biography, *Whom the Gods Love: The Story of Evariste Galois* (1948), describes how his work laid the foundations for Galois Theory and Group Theory – two major branches of abstract algebra. He was shot in the stomach on 30 May 1832 in a duel over a woman and died in the Hôpital Cochin the next day aged just 20.

The Cochin became a public hospital for the poor and a teaching centre. George Orwell, in his article, relates how, since he had a good example of a bronchial rattle, up to twenty students would line up in a queue to listen to his chest (Orwell 1970 [1946]: 264). Then would come ear after ear pressed against his back 'and relays of fingers solemnly but clumsily tapping. However, not from any one of them did you get a word of conversation or a look direct

JOHN P. LETHBRIDGE

in your face' (ibid). Medical students learnt their trade on the poor before they qualified and could look after the rich.

MARTHE HANAU – BACKGROUND AND EARLY LIFE

There were many French financial scandals between the two world wars. The most notorious was the Serge Stavisky affair which erupted after French Treasury Department officials uncovered an elaborate system of forged savings bonds that Stavisky had orchestrated behind the innocuous facade of a Basque country bank, the Crédit municipal de Bayonne. It led to riots in which 22 people were killed and toppled a French government in 1934 (Gunther 1936: 159-161).

The best account of Marthe Hanau's case in English is a two-part article by the American journalist Janet Flanner (1892-1978) published in the *New Yorker* on 26 August 1939 (pp 37-41) and 2 September (pp 35-38). Apart from the Stavisky and Hanau cases there were many other French financial scandals in this era.

Flanner briefly mentions the Aeropostale affair, a premature and over-ambitious plan for an airmail service between France and her colonies (Mary 2012); and there were other scandals surrounding, for instance, Albert Oustric, a waiter turned crooked entrepreneur and banker (see *New York Times Magazine*, 14 December 1930); the self-styled Baron Fernand Pacquement, a crooked banker (see *Le Petit Journal*, 19 January 1929); and Elie Gerard Sacazan (*Le Petit Parisien*, 10 February 1929), another crooked banker whose case forced the resignation of the French Minister of Justice, Eugène Raynaldy.[1] These schemes started as or developed into Ponzi schemes i.e. they paid dividends out of capital not profits. They flourished in the easy-going and expansionist 1920s and came to grief in the Great Depression.

Marthe Hanau was born in Paris in 1884. Her Jewish mother ran a Montmartre baby clothes shop. She initially studied to be a teacher and was a brilliant mathematician. In 1908, aged 24, she married Lazare Bloch whose family had done well in the jute trade (jute is used in sacking). Her mother gave her a 300,000 francs dowry but Bloch lost it on the stock market – after which Bloch and his wife divorced but remained business partners. In 1919, they set up a soap and perfume shop (Flanner, Part I: 37); and in 1925 a one-room Paris stockbroker's office i.e. a 'bucket shop' to use British stock market jargon (ibid: 38).

GLORY DAYS

Next, Marthe Hanau launched a newspaper, the *Gazette de France*, to promote her financial schemes. In 1927, she hired, as editor, Joseph Henri Jean Baptiste Pierre Audibert, generally known as Pierre Audibert. According to his French death certificate, he was born in 1881 in Tournecoupe, a village in southwest France. He became a reporter for *Le Petit Parisien*, a Paris daily paper, in 1905, and founded a weekly, *La Defense Maritime*, in 1912.[2] French military records show that he served in the French army in the First World War, was badly wounded and won the Croix de Guerre.

Audibert was appointed editor of *L'Information*, a Paris financial paper, in 1917; moved to be editor of *Le Radical* in Marseilles in 1918; in 1918, he helped found the Syndicat des Journalistes, the French equivalent of the National Union of Journalists, and in 1924 was appointed Chief of Staff to Anatole de Menzie, the Radical Socialist Minister of Finance from 1924 to 1925 and Minister of Education from 1925 to 1926.[3]

Audibert was, through de Menzie, an associate of Édouard Herriot, a Radical Socialist (ibid) who three times combined being Prime and Foreign Minister of France with being Mayor of Lyons from 1905 until his death in 1957. In 1928, the Kellogg-Briand Treaty was signed in Paris and named after the American Secretary of State Frank Billings Kellogg and the French Foreign Minister Aristide Briand. In it, 15 countries including France, Germany, Britain and the USA renounced the use of war as an instrument of foreign policy and agreed to settle any disputes by international arbitration (Thompson 2000).

Janet Flanner (Part I: 38) describes how Hanau and Audibert produced a special issue of the *Gazette de France* to celebrate the Kellogg-Briand Treaty. Audibert even obtained signed photographs of Briand; Raymond Nicholas Landry Poincaré, the then-French Prime Minister; Jean Louis Firmin Barthou and Joseph Paul-Boncour, both prominent French politicians; Miguel Primo de Rivera, the dictator of Spain from 1923 to 1930 (although King Alfonso XIII was the Spanish head of state); Benito Mussolini, the Italian dictator, and Cardinal Louis-Ernest Dubois, the Archbishop of Paris. They were published in this issue. But in getting such men involved with them Hanau and Audibert were living dangerously.

Because of Audibert's political connections, copies of this special issue were sent to all ambassadors in Europe and to all French schoolteachers. The diplomats realised that this was a publicity stunt by the politicians but many teachers were fooled that Hanau was a trustworthy person with whom to invest. The same issue offered investors in a wide variety of projects, from oil and textiles to South of France golf courses – with up to 40 per cent profits. Even her apparently normal investment bank, the Compagnie Générale Financière et Foncière, offered 8 per cent interest – well above the normal rate (Flanner, Part I: 38).

JOHN P. LETHBRIDGE

In 1928, Hanau obtained new grandiose Paris offices, employing 450 people there and with 175 agents elsewhere in France. Her ostensible business manager was the Count de Courville but he knew nothing about business. She ended up with 60,000 investors. As well as her main paper, she published a morning one predicting daily stock market developments and an evening journal explaining what had actually happened there. Her investors included priests, widows, retired officers, teachers and small shopkeepers (Flanner, Part I: 39).

Hanau paid herself 150,000 francs a month. She bought Chez les Zoaques, a Normandy country house, from Alexandre Georges Pierre Guitry, better known as Sacha Guitry, a famous French actor, playwright and director. She spent heavily on jewellery and gambled at Monte Carlo but normally wore drab clothes to avoid alarming her investors (ibid: 40).

THE FALL

In October 1928, Action Française, a French royalist group, called Hanau a swindler. In the following month, the French perfume manufacturer and newspaper tycoon François Coty's paper, *L'Ami du Peuple* repeated this accusation. Orwell's first published essay, in *G. K's Weekly*, on 29 December 1928, was actually a damning critique of the journal (Orwell 1968 [1928]). It was notoriously anti-semitic but Coty, an experienced businessman, knew that if an investment offer was too good to be true it probably was (Flanner, Part II: 35).

The Radical Socialist French government was alarmed. It was in financial trouble and about to offer a 3 per cent national loan. How could it compete with Hanau's 40 per cent projects or even her 8 per cent bank? On 3 December 1928, a special cabinet meeting discussed her case. The next day, she was arrested and thrown into St Lazare Prison, a Paris women's gaol (Flanner, Part I: 41; Hillairet 1956). Its former inmates included the alleged German spy Mata Hari. Hanau's ex-husband, Bloch, her editor Audibert and the Count de Courville were held in La Santé Prison, a Paris man's gaol (ibid).

Flanner (ibid) vividly describes how the French government's financial experts took less than an hour to discover that Hanau was a fraudster operating a Ponzi scheme and had paid dividends out of capital rather than profits. Her underwriters were usually her ex-husband – acting under false names. Her office staff were mainly young women chosen for looks not brains and she kept no proper financial records. All four prisoners were charged with fraud.

THE INSTRUCTION

French trials have two parts. In the first, known as the instruction, the prosecution, defence, experts, witnesses and prisoners offer to the instructing judge all the evidence they intend to use in the main trial. The instruction opened in January 1929 and lasted 16 months (ibid: 35). Hanau fought hard and sued nearly everyone who appeared in court including the judge after around 80 documents had gone missing from her desk since her arrest. And she attacked the French government's financial experts because, she said, they had made a mistake of 11,642,269 francs and 42 centimes in adding up her accounts. They proved that their error was only 10,924,708 francs and 28 centimes! Sometimes she was apparently kind to the experts: for instance, correcting their pencil and paper calculations of her accounts with accurate figures drawn from her memory.

Hanau's court antics amused the French newspaper-reading public but there was a sadder aspect to her case. Several of the investors she had ruined killed themselves. Flanner describes several cases including a miller of Chambéry, in southeast France, who shot and killed his spinster sister and then shot himself. With their life savings gone they faced penury (ibid).

French fraudsters were not usually gaoled while awaiting trial. In the most notorious case, Serge Stavisky was arrested in 1926 but provisionally released. The Paris Prosecutor postponed Stavisky's trial 19 times until the case became public knowledge and Stavisky killed himself in January 1934 (Gunther 1936).

THE HÔPITAL COCHIN AGAIN

Audibert claimed to have angina while in gaol. The Count de Courville, unused to cold cells, developed pneumonia but recovered (Flanner, Part 11: 35). Flanner describes how Hanau went on hunger strike in March 1930 after months in gaol. On day 23, it was decided to force feed her and she was taken to the Hôpital Cochin's prison ward. But she stubbornly resisted – biting through a half-inch rubber feeding tube and smashing two stoneware cups before succumbing.

After two days in the hospital Hanau escaped. Her maid, Marie Snoeck, bought her a coat, a linen sheet and money. Hanau, in her nightclothes and the coat, squeezed through a window and slid down the sheet. She hailed a cab and drove to a post office where she sent a letter to the Minister of Justice threatening a law suit. She then hailed another cab and asked the driver to take her to Santé Lazare Prison. He took two wrong turnings so she paid him off to avoid being twisted any further. She went into a bistro and telephoned her lawyer telling him about the force feeding. She then took another cab back to the prison, giving the driver a generous tip and handing herself in at the prison gates. She resumed her hunger strike and came close to death. Two days after her return to gaol she was freed on 800,000 francs bail, half of it being provided by her creditors. The French government did not want to create a martyr.

THE MAIN TRIAL

Hanau's main trial opened in October 1930 after she had recovered her health. The judge's opening accusation took three hours to read. Again she fought hard, defending her business methods and claiming they were democratic – unlike the elitist large banks. She even claimed that her alleged accomplices were just office boys (ibid: 36).

On 28 March 1931, Hanau was convicted of fraud and sentenced to two years in gaol. Her ex-husband, Bloch, was sentenced to 18 months. Audibert was acquitted but on 30 March 1931 he dropped dead at his Paris home aged 49.[4] The Count de Courville was acquitted having proved that Hanau had defrauded him of 500,000 francs. His wife then sued him for separation because it was her money that he had lost (ibid).

FREE ON APPEAL

Hanau appealed against her sentence in April 1931 and was freed to await the result. She set up a new office and went into business again and paid her creditors 40 per cent of what she owed them. She set up a new financial paper, *Le Secret des Dieux*, and quickly secured 2,000 subscribers (ibid).

Hanau bitterly criticised big business. In one year, of the 27 stocks she recommended, 20 soared, four did respectably well, while one performed badly – a good record for a stock tipster (ibid: 37). She could certainly spot swindlers. For instance, on 9 March 1932, she warned that the Swedish entrepreneur, Ivar Kreuger, was heading for trouble. He committed suicide in Paris three days later.

In July 1934, the Paris Court of Appeals heard Hanau's case and raised her sentence to three years. She appealed against the extra year but on 22 February 1935 the Appeal Court's sentence was confirmed. Three hours later she was arrested and returned to gaol (ibid).

THE END

On her arrest, the French police confiscated a revolver from Hanau but she obtained Veronal sleeping pills. On the evening of Monday 15 July 1935, she took an overdose in her cell and died the next day aged 51. In her last letter to her lawyer, she said that she was sick of money which had crushed her and that she wished to be cremated (ibid: 38).

Hanau's death was announced by the French authorities on Friday 19 July 1935. According to French law, as she had died violently she could not be cremated. She was buried in Montparnasse Cemetery in Paris where many other notable people were buried including the poet Charles Pierre Baudelaire (1821-1867). The same year that Hanau died Major Alfred Dreyfus, a famous victim of injustice, was buried there.

CONCLUSION

The Hôpital Cochin still exists, has a website and houses Paris's Central Burns Unit. Since 1990, a biomedical research centre, the Institut Cochin, has been associated with it. In 2002, this centre was reorganised to include genetic research, molecular biology work and cellular biology work. The Prison Santé Lazare, where Hanau was held, was demolished in late 1935. Only the chapel and infirmary survived as part of the hospital which replaced the prison. They are listed historic buildings (Hillairet 1956).

La Santé, where Hanau's male associates were held, is today one of France's most notorious prisons (Vasseur 2000) and has high security and VIP wings. During the Second World War, 18 French resistance fighters were executed there and many Algerians were held there during the Algerian war of independence (1954-1962). Montparnasse Cemetery is today a tourist attraction and features in the 2019 *Michelin Guide* to Paris. People buried there since 1935 include the philosopher Jean-Paul Sartre and his lover, Simone de Beauvoir.

BACK TO YOU GEORGE

When Orwell mentioned Hanau in his article he was writing 11 years after she had died and working from memory. Yet her story vividly illustrates the corruption of Third Republic France which Orwell refers to in some of his other writings such as 'The Lion and the Unicorn' where he says (1968 [1941]: 88):

> Is the English press honest or dishonest? At normal times it is deeply dishonest. All the papers that matter live off their advertisements, and the advertisers exercise an indirect censorship over news. Yet I do not suppose there is one paper in England that can be straight-forwardly bribed with hard cash. In the France of the Third Republic all but a very few of the newspapers could notoriously be bought over the counter like so many pounds of cheese.

ACKNOWLEDGEMENTS

Copies of Janet Flanner's two-part *New Yorker* article were obtained from the British Library though determined attempts to contact her estate were all in vain. Information came from many other sources.

JOHN P. LETHBRIDGE

Special thanks go to the British Library, the Bibliothèque Nationale de France, Josephine Huet, a professional genealogist who found and translated much material in France, Tristan Gaston Breton, a busy man who supplied valuable information, particularly about Pierre Audibert and the Sacazan Bank, and Jackie Cotterill, of the Midland Ancestors Group.

NOTES

[1] Tristan Gaston Breton, email to author, 5 January 2019

[2] Information from Tristan Gaston Breton and the Bibliothèque Nationale de France

[3] Ibid

[4] His death certificate, obtained and translated by Josephine Huet

REFERENCES

Breton, Tristan Gaston, email 5 January 2019

Flanner, Janet (1939) Annals of Crime – The Swindling Presidente, *New Yorker*, 26 August and 2 September

Gillies, Stewart, British Library, email, 4 March 2019

Gunther, John (1936) *Inside Europe*, London: Hamish Hamilton, fifth edition

Hillairet, Jacques (1956) *Gibets, Pilories et Cachots du Vieux Paris*, Paris: editions de Minuit

Herbermann, Charles (1913) *Catholic Encyclopaedia*, New York: Encyclopaedia Press

Infeld, Leopold (1948) *Whom the Gods Love: The Story of Évariste Galois*, London: McGraw Hill

Mary, Jack (2012) *Aeropostale, Les Autres Lines*, Paris: Privat

Orwell, George (1968 [1928]) A farthing newspaper, Orwell, Sonia and Angus, Ian (eds) *The Collected Essays, Journalism and Letters, Vol. 1: An Age Like This 1920-1940*, London: Penguin pp 34-37

Orwell, George (1968 [1941]) The Lion and the Unicorn, Orwell, Sonia and Angus, Ian (eds) *The Collected Essays, Journalism and Letters, Vol. 2: My Country Right or Left, 1940-1943*, London: Penguin pp 74-134

Orwell, George (1968 [1946]) How the poor die, Orwell, Sonia and Angus, Ian (eds) *The Collected Essays, Journalism and Letters, Vol. 4: In Front of Your Nose, 1945-1950*, London: Penguin pp 261-272; original published in *Now*

Thompson, Peter (2000) *Cassell's Dictionary of Modern American History*, London: Cassell & Co.

Vasseur, Véronique (2000) *Médecin-chef à la Prison de la Santé*, Paris: Le Cherche Midi

NOTE ON THE CONTRIBUTOR

John P. Lethbridge is an independent researcher, historian, author, small publisher and public speaker. His book, *Foul Deeds & Suspicious Deaths in Warwickshire*, was published by Wharncliffe in 2007 and is still in print. Of his self-published books, *The Soldier's Reward, Birmingham in the First World War* and *Victorian Birmingham* are still in print.

ARTICLE

Thoughtcrime ...
im Zimmer 101

A year after German reunification, John Rodden led a class in Leipzig on *Nineteen Eighty-Four*. Here he describes how a utopian inversion of the Two Minutes Hate suddenly erupted as the students loudly echoed in German the novel's Newspeak slogans. 'It's pandemonium – a momentary reminder of a fast-disappearing world of solidarity and hope and fun.'

Leipzig, 20 October 1991. Karl Marx University. First stop on my peripatetic second tour of East German university and gymnasium classrooms since German reunification the previous October. The assignment for today? Unthinkable less than two years ago: George Orwell's *Nineteen Eighty-Four*. *Endlich mal*! At last! This is a moment about which I have secretly dreamed, if not schemed, for a decade.

Until now, though I've been invited to teach several classes in history, literature or civics to East German schoolchildren and university pupils, the topics have always been part of the prescribed curriculum (which was rigid even at the university level) – albeit from the 'Western' or 'American' perspective, as my hosts have encouraged. During the *ancien régime*, however unfathomable such an invitation would have been (except possibly as a debating exercise exhibiting Marxist-Leninist dialectics), the 'Western perspective' would have meant the (retrograde) 'bourgeois' or 'neo-imperialist' viewpoint.

My curricular topics? Leading off with the Berlin airlift of 1947-1948 and the construction of the Berlin Wall in 1961, we proceed to the literary and philosophical substance of formerly *verboten* 'cosmopolitans', 'aesthetes', theists and outright anti-socialists and fascist Germans exalted in the West (for instance, Spengler, Rilke, Luther, Nietzsche).

Now, however, I am standing in front of my Leipzig class of English majors, cradling an English-language copy of *Nineteen Eighty-Four* – or rather *1984* (i.e., the emblazoned Signet paperback title, reflecting the abridged, digitised, quasi-Newspeak American usage). It is not lost on any of us that we owe this encounter partly to the fact that *1984* had led to 1989 – and to the still-onrushing whoosh of events since then. Yes, it's a new world since the *Wende* (the 'Turn').

II

In the year since reunification on 3 October 1990, like everything else in Eastern Germany during the past months, anarchy reigns in higher education. Everything is in a state of uncertainty and upheaval. No textbooks, no established curricula in many institutions. Entire departments are threatened with closure (*Abwicklung*, 'wrapping up', in the Newspeak of Western German officialdom) because their faculties and staff consist chiefly of Communist Party members and also quite a few secret police (or so-called *Stasi* agents). Every professor is undergoing a *haargenaue Überprüfung* (razor-close screening or evaluation), both according to scholarly and ideological criteria. With mountains of now-available *Stasi* dossiers in the hands of Western German educators, professors fear the worst. Unless you come through with a *weisse weste* ('white vest', an immaculate record), your career is *kaput*.

'It's a witch hunt,' a young *dozent* whispers to me. He means a Red Scare, Teutonic-style. (I have come to learn that having a Western sympathiser, especially an American – the former erstwhile ideological enemy – may be looked upon favourably by the West German evaluators.) True enough, professors are being summarily fired, especially in 'ideologically sensitive' (a.k.a. Marxist-Leninist or propagandistic) subjects such as philosophy, history, literature, sociology and political science.

So everyone, and most especially any formerly high-ranking member of the Communist Party, was quite delighted to be associated with a Western professor who was known not only in America and Britain but in West Germany for his work about an outspoken anti-communist such as George Orwell. Whereas I was not even granted entry to the country a couple of years earlier, I am now welcomed everywhere I go in the 'wild East'.

As I lunch with the editorial collective of the *Zeitschrift für Anglistik und Amerikanistik*, the leading quarterly devoted to English-language literature and culture in the GDR, I am reminded that my recently published article on *1984* in the *ZAA* had actually been accepted shortly before the fall of the Berlin Wall. The longtime editor, the genial Helmut Findeisen, and his colleagues are proud of this fact, which testifies to the excellent judgment and political courage of the editors. (Perhaps I might draw this to the attention of my West German contacts?)

After lunch we all head over to the advanced class of undergraduate English majors. We've been chatting in German, and I sense that the English facility of some of the professors is shaky (particularly those who had not been privileged to travel to the West). 'Be patient with our students,' a professor says, taking me aside. 'They are still learning English.' '*Selbstverstandlich*' I assure him. 'Of course.'

III

Yes, this is a moment about which I've dreamed. Throughout the mid-1980s, I harboured a strong desire that resembled George Orwell's own wish four decades earlier to witness World War Two and glimpse the emergence of the postwar era. I was studying Orwell's life and times, and I felt as though I was entering deeply into his imagination, both political and personal. As he had yearned to do, I longed to witness first-hand what might be the major, indeed world-historical, international event of my lifetime: the fall of the Berlin Wall, the collapse of communism and dawn of a post-communist age. I wanted to see 'really existing socialism' in Eastern Europe while it was still really existing, that is, before the march of Western capitalism swept it all away like the post-World War Two rubble that still was, even in the early 1980s, still visible in a few city streets in some provincial towns of East Germany.

Beginning in the mid-1980s, every time I applied to the Ministry of Travel in East Germany – officially known as the German Democratic Republic (GDR) – I was politely informed that my application was 'still under consideration'. As the East Berlin bureaucrats doubtless intended, since they knew that I was a professor who could not remain in Europe beyond the end of my summer or Christmas vacation visits, the endless delays inevitably meant that I had to return home to the USA without receiving approval. (A trip to East Berlin, which was usually quite expensive and gave the communist government much-coveted hard currency of West German marks, was not a problem. But East Berlin offered little more than a showcase tour; one's freedom of movement was tightly restricted and one could not venture beyond the officially approved tourist areas.) I wanted to travel in the hinterlands, for which official permission from the Ministry of Travel was necessary. I had received invitations from colleagues there; one invariably needed such invitations in order to travel outside East Berlin at all.

I knew that my chances for permission to travel inside East Germany were marginal, at best. They rested largely on my hope that the bureaucratic inefficiency of the GDR's surveillance octopus had rendered the watchdogs unaware of my suspect profile – that is, as a skeptic of 'really existing' socialism in the GDR. Might my published work escape their notice? My application specified that my invitations were from ordinary East Germans who would welcome 'an American friend' of their long-unseen relatives in West Germany (and not issued by university professors or GDR intellectuals). I worried because, after all, I had been publishing articles on Orwell and his view of socialism, along with numerous other essays that expressed a dim view of Soviet communism (e.g., about the ex-Trotskyist, anti-Soviet *Partisan Review* intellectuals). As it turned out, I learned after the fall of the Wall that my writings on Orwell had, indeed, rendered me *persona non grata*.

ARTICLE

JOHN RODDEN Not until after the Wall fell in November 1989 did I set foot in the rapidly crumbling GDR. And the ferment in the fields was evident to me in every step.

So at long last, like Orwell, I too was granted my wish to travel for an on-site inspection of world history in the making – or rather, unmaking. Yes, Orwell and I were granted our wishes, albeit in very different ways. David Astor, publisher of the London *Observer*, sent Orwell to liberated Paris and occupied Germany as the war was winding down in the spring of 1945. Likewise, after the Berlin Wall fell, yet before German reunification in October 1990, I was finally able – without regard for official approval – to travel to what was still the 'GDR'. It proved to be an eye-opening, even astounding experience.

I have written at length in several books about my adventures and misadventures in the GDR. But I have never mentioned a small yet fascinating episode involving *1984* during a trip to Karl Marx University, as it was still called at the time, in Leipzig. (Soon the university would return to its pre-communist name, Leipzig University.)

IV

Back to the classroom on 20 October 1991. Despite the (understandable) linguistic deficiencies of the English professors at the Karl Marx University, my colleagues mention again – implicitly by way of apology – that all classes in *Anglistik und Amerikanistik* are conducted in the English language even if the students' command of the language is poor. As I begin, I am careful to speak at a slower rate than normal and to weave in several synonyms to assist comprehension of vocabulary that might prove daunting.

And then a strange thing happens. As I begin to lecture about Newspeak and its references to wartime Britain and Europe, whispers pass throughout the room. At first, I ignore them; in any case, I haven't heard clearly what the students are saying to each other as I speak. Courtesy, I feel, dictates that I do not make an issue of what seems to be an impolite interruption.

As I continue my discussion of Orwell's coinages and catchwords, the whispering across the aisles grows louder. Suddenly I hear German words that I recognise. I realise that a few knowledgeable students are translating Orwell's coinages into German for their struggling classmates.

Then a lovely and surprising turn of events occurs – triggering an interaction that every teacher would doubtless cherish. Intending to assist the students by following my every mention of a Newspeak locution with a German version of Orwell's neologism (in those

West German translations with which I was familiar), I suddenly find the entire class repeat them aloud – with the gathering force of a collective chant.

What ensues is a joyous cascade of Two Minutes Love, as it were, a utopian inversion of Orwell's Two Minutes Hate. For every one of the novel's slogans, the students echo me – and, in some instances, 'correct' me by shouting out translation variants more familiar to East Germans. And so it all proceeds:

>'Big Brother Is Watching You!' *Der Große Bruder sieht dich an*!
>
>'Newspeak!' *Neusprech*!
>
>'Doublethink!' *Doppelsinnigkeit*! (*Nein*, erupts a voice from the rear. *Zweidenken*!) Then the class's acknowledgment that the latter translation is the preferred one: *Jawohl*!)
>
>'Thoughtcrime!' *Gedankenverbrechen*!
>
>'Thought criminal!' *Gedankenverbrecher*!
>
>'The Brotherhood.' *Die Bruderschaft*!
>
>'Memory hole.' *Der Gedächtnisloch*!
>
>'Down with Big Brother!' *Nieder mit dem Großen Bruder*!
>
>'War Is Peace!' *Krieg ist Friede*!
>
>'Freedom Is Slavery!' *Freiheit bedeutet Sklaverei*!
>
>'Ignorance Is Strength!' *Unwissenheit ist Stärke*!

A theatrical student – the same fellow who had cried out the East German lingo for doublethink – opens his arms wide as he gestures to the four walls. 'Room 101!' he shouts. '*Zimmer 101*!' echoes the class. Given the rigid, repressive standards of address and behaviour that have traditionally governed German (above all East German) classrooms, it's pandemonium – a momentary reminder of a fast-disappearing world of solidarity and hope and fun, of a misty near-past when the defiant, confident chants against the Party *bonzen* (bigwigs) reverberated through the streets of every GDR city and town. It recalls the wondrous feeling of community, the brief advent of *really* existing socialism that – *endlich mal*! – at long last prevailed in that *annus mirabilis* of 1989-1990, captured forever in the twilight revelry of triumphant, joyous, Dionysian dancing atop the Wall on the night of 9 November, two light years ago.

In a spirit of 'last but not least', I wave my copy of the novel before the class as I call out: '1984!'

>*Neunzehnhundertvierundachtzig*!

V

As we finish the litany, still chuckling, I ask the students how they know all these slogans so well. 'The novel was banned in all your

JOHN RODDEN bookstores for decades – just like the "Nazi" Nietzsche,' I observe. I add that I've been told that no library allowed any unauthorised patron to look at such a book. Professors have informed me that the work of Orwell, Arthur Koestler, André Gide and numerous other allegedly anti-socialist, anti-progressive 'enemies of The People' were identified in GDR library card catalogues by a red dot. The red dot signified that they were on a restricted list available only to senior Communist Party officials or specifically authorised researchers (who periodically cited Orwell et al. for ritualistic denunciation). Colloquially, such books were said to be on the *giftschrank* ('poison shelf').

'So how did you know all these slogans from the book – in German?' I ask. 'They were regularly in the headlines and in the lead paragraph of the party newspaper, *Neues Deutschland* [the *New Germany*],' one student replies. Another student notes that the catchwords were used 'to describe *your* political leaders and capitalist system'. I laugh and nod. *Na ja. Selbstverstandlich*. Of course. 'So you knew that Ronald Reagan was Big Brother,' I continue. 'And Margaret Thatcher was Big Sister,' another student adds.

I quiz the class on the other references to Britain and the US, several of which they have been unaware. I draw their attention to Orwell's cautionary warning to the West: 'Don't let it happen. It depends on you.' His references signaling the book's application to the West are strewn throughout the novel. Oceania is America (or 'Amerika'), Airstrip One is London – and references to the Oceania currency of dollars, to Victory cigarettes and, of course, to Ingsoc (English socialism). A few students vaguely recall that these allusions also appeared occasionally in official GDR contexts to 'enlighten' readers that the capitalist world was really the anti-utopian 'evil empire'.

So – irony of ironies – even though *1984* was banned from GDR bookshops and unavailable in the library stacks, its slogans nonetheless were widely known in the republic, thanks to the unremitting efforts of GDR propagandists. I knew that some East Germans were acquainted with *1984*. During the 1980s, I had interviewed a few men and women, now in the West, who had committed *republikflucht* ('escape from the republic') and fled to West Berlin. They told me that they were familiar with the language and vision of his novel. Generally speaking, however, these interviewees were dissidents – and often intellectuals – who had read *samizdat* and been closely in touch with fellow renegades and heretics. By contrast, to encounter a classroom full of young people aware of Orwell's coinages in their native tongue – let alone in my first experience of teaching *1984* outside the West – that stunned me. As it does still to this day, nearly three decades later. It remains my radiant and enduring East German *sternstunde*, a glorious, unforgettable experience, an exalted moment fixed in eternity.

From an educator's and historian's standpoint, this little episode also represents a choice instance of the 'Orwellian' pedagogical methods that prevailed in the GDR, an enduring testament to the (unfortunate) didactic prowess of the so-called Ministry of Propaganda and Enlightenment, which set 'agitprop' policy for the state-controlled media. And equally powerful evidence of the boundless cynicism of the regime's Communist Party apparatchniks towards the GDR's 'proles' who 're-elected' the one-party slate to power in 'yet another overwhelming landslide' (indeed: 99.6 per cent in the – unexpectedly – last election of June 1989), all of it further proof that the invincible party spoke for *das Volk*.

VI

Today, thirty years after the fall of the Berlin Wall, I ask myself: 'What might George Orwell have said about all this?' He was certainly no political naïf. He was well aware that his work could be abused towards unforeseen ends – and, indeed, was being exploited for anti-socialist purposes. Informed that *Animal Farm* was being translated and distributed by right-wing polemicists in Germany and brandished against socialist 'pigs' – and also misleadingly presented as anti-socialist by some American reviewers – Orwell sought to prevent it happening with *1984*. On his deathbed in 1949, he issued a *dementi* to the American press protesting over attempts by adherents of 'one hundred per cent Americanism' to cast Ingsoc, the ruling party in Oceania, as an ex-socialist's parting shot against the UK's ruling Labour Party.

Would Orwell have deplored the GDR's hijacking his language and twisting his vision to apply exclusively to the West? Undoubtedly so. Yet I like to imagine he would also have been consoled to learn how our class at Karl Marx University unfolded that beautiful autumn afternoon. I like to imagine he would have been gratified that the students proved so keen to engage in a wide-ranging discussion of his great novel and its application to both West and East, both his era and our own.

Above all, I like to imagine he would have been proud to hear the ebullient lovefest underway that day in *Zimmer 101*, as the Two Minutes Love chants echoed through the hallways.

Yes, it's as if those shouts of joy represented ecstatic rejoinders to the chorus of cries in the streets below three decades earlier, when peaceful protesters cradled candles as they marched quietly in the demonstrations of the *Revolution der Kerzen* (Revolution of the Candles) and a half-million voices exclaimed in unison: *WIR sind Das Volk*! WE are The People!

JOHN RODDEN NOTE ON THE CONTRIBUTOR

John Rodden has written four books on the politics and culture of modern Germany in the 20th century, along with several dozen articles on East German communism, the legacy of World War II, the prospects of post-communism, and the crimes against human rights under Nazism and Stalinism. His most recent book is *George Orwell: Life and letters, Legend and Legacy* (Princeton University Press, 2020).

ARTICLE

How TB Can be Traced in 'Forgotten' Spanish Civil War Letter

Gleb Zilberstein, Svetlana Zilberstein and Pier Giorgio Righetti

We are an international research initiative from Italy and Israel engaged in the study of microflora, human metabolites and other biochemical traces left on the pages of manuscripts, correspondence and personal belongings of historical people. This allows us to obtain objective molecular information about the person, the period of time and the environment surrounding the author. We came up with the idea to study Orwell's correspondence after and during the Civil War in Spain in connection with the need to understand his real state of health and compare the types of tuberculosis from Spanish hospitals with the strain that contaminated Orwell.

The war in Spain was the last modern war without penicillin and antibiotics. Therefore, mortality from infections after injuries was very high. In the Russian, British and Spanish archives, a large number of documents relating to the medical services of International Brigades are stored. Therefore, there was no shortage of material. Before Orwell's tuberculosis project, we examined the causes of Anton Chekhov's death. The work was carried out jointly with the A. Chekhov Museum in Melikhovo (near Moscow). The results are published in the journal *Proteomics*.[1]

The study of tuberculosis before the era of antibiotics is a very important area. Search and analysis of traces in correspondence permits us to obtain molecular information about infections of the past very effectively. This is important for medicine, pharmaceuticals, history and other fields. There are a lot of 'dark areas' in Orwell's biography. For example, many documents relating to Orwell, his wife and his comrades in arms, appear to be stored in Russian archives (such as the Russian State Archive of Social Political History). It would be good for historians to pay more attention to these documents. In the Russian archives, there is a treasury of absolutely astounding documents of the Comintern and the International Brigades. For example, the archives of Trotskyist organisations have not been thoroughly studied.

GLEB ZILBERSTEIN

SVETLANA ZILBERSTEIN

PIER GIORGIO RIGHETTIN

An interesting document we traced is a letter that Orwell sent to USSR on 2 July 1937. Its recipient was Sergey Sergeyevich Dinamov (real name Oglodkov, 16 September 1901, Moscow-16 April 1939) – Soviet literary critic, Shakespeare translator to Russian, editor of the journal *Foreign Literature*. Arrested on 26 September 1938, he was convicted by the Military Collegium of the Supreme Court of the USSR on 15 April 1939 on charges of participating in a counter-revolutionary terrorist organisation. He was shot and buried at the Kommunarka special facility in the Moscow Region but was later rehabilitated on 19 May 1956.

Dinamov wanted to translate into Russian Orwell's *The Road to Wigan Pier*. Orwell responded favourably but was quite frank about his allegiances during the Spanish Civil War and did not want the publisher to have problems with the Communist Party and other Soviet authorities. In his own words:

> I must tell you that in Spain I was serving in the militia of the POUM which, as you no doubt know, has been bitterly denounced by the Communist Party and was recently suppressed by the Government. ... I tell you this because it may be that your paper would not care to have contributions from a POUM member, and I do not wish to introduce myself to you under false pretences.

Dinamov did not go ahead with the translation.

The letter is stored in the Russian State Archive of Literature and Art in Moscow. In the case of Orwell's letter, we found six proteins characteristic of tuberculosis pathogens from various republican hospitals in Spain. We explored the surface of this letter page via a technology we have developed, known by the acronym EVA (ethylene vinyl acetate studded with strong anion and cation exchangers as well as with hydrophobic resins) (Righetti et al. 2019, 2020).[2]

The biological material captured was analysed by mass spectrometry and, indeed, robust traces of six proteins specific for the Koch bacillus (*Mycobacterium tuberculosis*) could be found, namely: β-lactamase class-A, Proteasome subunit α/β, DNA topoisomerase type IIA subunit A/C-terminal, Isocitrate lyase, 19kDa lipoprotein antigen and 8-amino-7-oxononanoate synthase. It is remarkable that one could detect such proteins in an 83-year old document.[3]

It can thus be seen that precious documents stored into public archives and libraries can hold biological traces of their authors, invisible to historians and literature scholars who can only try to interpret the written text.[4]

NOTES

1 https://onlinelibrary.wiley.com/doi/abs/10.1002/pmic.201700447

2 https://pubs.acs.org/doi/abs/10.1021/acs.jproteome.0c00080 and https://www.tandfonline.com/doi/abs/10.1080/14789450.2019.1624164

3 https://onlinelibrary.wiley.com/doi/abs/10.1002/elps.202000063

4 https://www.newyorker.com/magazine/2018/11/26/do-proteins-hold-the-key-to-the-past and https://www.tandfonline.com/doi/full/10.1080/0950236X.2020.1786719 and https://www.sciencehistory.org/distillations/the-death-of-anton-chekhov-told-in-proteins and https://pubs.acs.org/doi/10.1021/acs.jproteome.0c00080

NOTE ON THE CONTRIBUTORS

Gleb Zilberstein is an employee of Spectrophon Ltd, Oppenheimer 7, Rehovot, 7670107, Israel. Svetlana Zilberstein works in the Spectrophon Ltd, Oppenheimer 7, Rehovot, 7670107, Israel. Pier Giorgio Righetti works in the Politecnico di Milano, Via Mancinelli 7, Milano 20131, Italy.

ARTICLE

FILM REVIEW

The Hunt Reduces Orwell, Yet Again, to a Meme Theme

Benedict Cooper, in reviewing a new slasher-cum-satirical movie, highlights the way in which the author of *Animal Farm* is constantly appropriated by both left and right in the 'culture wars'.

'You've read *Animal Farm*?' So asks the female villain of *The Hunt*, Blumhouse's slasher-cum-satirical film to the unlikely heroine, a Mississippi hick she's nicknamed Snowball. As she learns to her cost, during their showdown, she has a bad case of cognitive bias. Despite Snowball's lowly identity – in the eyes of her hunter at least – our heroine, real name Crystal, has read a book or two.

Briefly, the background and the premise of the film: Crystal is the last survivor of a human hunt that targets a group of ignorant, right-wing 'deplorables' – Trump supporters, in short – who have been kidnapped by left-wing elites, transported to a hidden location and let loose on the countryside.

The prey is a sample of everything liberal America loves to hate: the NRA gun-toter, the Westboro Baptist Church homophobe, the right-wing shock-jock – a thinly veiled parody of Alex Jones – the trailer-trash beatnik, the big-game trophy hunter, and so on. When he heard about the film, Donald Trump issued a Tweet attacking 'liberal Hollywood' for making a movie which, he said, was 'made in order to inflame and cause chaos'.

For me, it was more like tasting a sickly cocktail of leftovers from the last few years of cultural and political discourse. As a member of the committee of The Orwell Society, what rang alarm bells was the film's Orwell fetish. It crawls with casual references to *Animal Farm* and *Nineteen Eighty-Four*.

The hunt, for instance, takes place in the grounds of Manor House (Manor Farm is where *Animal Farm* is set), and the name of the 'mom and pop store' in which the hunted take shelter is Willington's (Manor Farm is near the town of Willingdon). Early in the film, one of the hunters, fresh from bludgeoning a hick, declares 'War is war' (a line from *Animal Farm*). I've already mentioned Snowball, and the chat about Orwell's novel. And, just to make sure nothing at all is left to your imagination, there's a pig on the loose – called Orwell.

To be fair, *The Hunt* doesn't take itself too seriously. But it does take a stab at commenting on the state of polarised political debate in the US, and, to an extent, the West as a whole. Yet it's such a confused message that it's hard to tell if *The Hunt* is critiquing the all-too-common phenomenon of citing Orwell as some trump card in a debate, or whether it's guilty of this lazy tendency itself.

It often feels like the latter. The references don't bear scrutiny. The Snowball character in Orwell's novel is universally accepted as an allegory for Leon Trotsky, in the context of a post-Revolution power struggle, not merely some vague hero or 'idealist'. And in the film, the hunters are achingly woke, powerful elites who check each other's privileges (one tells another that he shouldn't wear a kimono because it's 'appropriation').

FILM REVIEW

But it only takes a cursory reading of *Animal Farm* to know that the pig Napoleon, fighting it out with Snowball for control of the farm, represents Stalin – hardly a woke icon. And at the same time, on the Left it's more on-message to contrast Orwell's Napoleon with Donald Trump.

You'd think it impossible that writers Nick Cuse and Damon Lindelof didn't know all this. But there's an extraordinary preponderance in Western culture of citing, quoting and evoking Orwell with only the thinnest understanding of his works.

At an event I attended last year, for example, to promote *The Ministry of Truth*, Dorian Lynskey's major new 'biography' of *Nineteen Eighty-Four*, an audience member raised their hand and asked whether the author would agree that the modern world had become 'just like in *Nineteen Eighty-Four*', before admitting: 'I haven't actually read the book, but...'

Orwell's mass popularity and revival in modern discourse as an omni-prescient figure has also been his curse. Seventy years after his death, and with many of the copyrights on his works soon to expire, he's in a state of being continuously claimed, appropriated and evoked. And both sides of the political divide are at it.

So, in modern Britain, it's possible (supposedly) that to implore students to report 'micro-aggressions' on campus is an 'Orwellian attempt to silence free speech', and that the expulsion of Labour members for alleged anti-Semitism is also 'all very Orwellian'.

BENEDICT COOPER

In promoting his newly-formed Free Speech Union, meanwhile, journalist Toby Young, who loves to rail against the left, has resorted to one of the most commonly-cited Orwell quotes – 'If liberty means anything at all, it means the right to tell people what they don't want to hear' – happily overlooking its author's fundamental left-wing politics.

It's conspicuous in the American presidential campaign, too. The alt-left media across the Atlantic say that 'the anti-Sanders attack machine has taken an Orwellian turn', while veteran CBS News anchor Dan Rather contends that what Orwell wrote is 'practically a shooting script for Trump', a man who's 'trying to move us into an Orwellian space where truth doesn't matter and the opposite of truth is truth'.

This state of affairs has long been the case. Even when Orwell was alive, he was claimed and counter-claimed by opposing sides. But the tendency has reached absurd proportions in these febrile modern times, the *zeitgeist* of which *The Hunt* is trying so hard to capture.

It comes down to your idea of what a dystopia would look like: whether Big Brother would be the authoritarian force that looms over all, suffocating free speech in the name of the collective good, or the warmongering enslaver who crushes individuals and teaches hate and mistrust. The right tends to focus on Orwell's defence of free speech and anti-Communist positions, while the left cites vivid attacks on nationalism, colonialism and the injustices of the English class system.

But to reduce Orwell to a meme theme, and his great works and thoughts to tick-offs on a game of cultural buzzword bingo, is to inflict a painful historical irony on a writer who, above all, loathed precisely this sort of casuistry, and the cheap 'swindles and perversions' of language to which he himself is now subjected.

We can be glad that Orwell is alive in the collective mind. But we should be wary of the price that he, and we, may have to pay for the privilege.

- Thanks to the *Daily Telegraph* for allowing us to re-publish this review.

NOTE ON THE CONTRIBUTOR

Benedict Cooper is a freelance journalist and member of The Orwell Society committee.

BOOK REVIEWS

Eileen: The Making of George Orwell
Sylvia Topp
Unbound, London, 2020, pp 475
ISBN: 978 1 7835 2708 3 (hbk)

This biography seeks to uncover the largely hidden history of Eileen O'Shaughnessy, Orwell's first wife and his greatest editor, advocate and, if author Sylvia Topp is right, muse and co-writer. It brings to light new stories and documents, and analyses documents that receive cursory treatment in other studies. Hers is the first biography to cite in full a 1934 poem by Eileen titled 'End of the Century: 1984,' and to have digested the contents of Eileen's letters from the mid-1930s to her good friend Norah Symes Myles that surfaced in 2005. Her sedulous research has also yielded visual contents – rare photographs of Eileen as a teenager, of her relatives, homes, and friends – that also enrich Orwell's story.

Topp believes that Orwell titled his last novel in honour of Eileen and her poem although, after reading hundreds of pages documenting Orwell's indifference to Eileen's education, her career, her interests, her feelings, her time, her comfort and her health, readers may be forgiven for concluding that Orwell simply and perhaps unconsciously appropriated the poem's subtitle to serve his own purposes.

The question of what exactly inspired the title of *Nineteen Eighty-Four* – was it an act of memorial or appropriation – will not be settled unless we uncover more documents attesting to the history of motives of the parties involved. More to the point, Eileen's poem is not a particularly good one; without its connection to Orwell's last, great work, it would not serve as evidence of Eileen's hypothesised destiny as a literary figure in her own right. And this gestures towards a central dilemma of Topp's project. Topp wants to recover Eileen for literary history, to restore her as an active and equal partner in Orwell's work and willing co-creator of a free marriage, but these admirable goals have to be achieved through evidence that suggests Eileen's life as an autonomous person was for the most part consumed by endless domestic drudgery and unpaid secretarial service to George Orwell.

The effects of this unresolvable dilemma are felt in matters large and small, from the structure of the biography to Topp's interpretation of minor anecdotes. For example, in the chapter titled 'Six Happy Months of Marriage', we read an excerpt from the first extant letter by Eileen sent to Norah Symes Myles and preserved in that precious batch of correspondence discovered in 2005. Eileen writes: 'I lost my habit of punctual correspondence during the first few weeks of marriage because we quarreled so continuously & really bitterly that I thought I'd save time & just write one letter to everyone when the murder or separation had been accomplished' (pp 138-139). Eileen describes to Norah the two-month visit of Orwell's Aunt Nellie to the newlyweds, the Wallington cottage oven that wouldn't cook anything, the smoking hearth, the continual rain, the flooded kitchen floor, to which picture we could add, as Topp does, the unremittingly hard labour of tending garden, chickens and goats. Other sources cited in the chapter suggest, on top of these damp miseries, sexual estrangement and physical and psychic separation. Topp's conclusion that these months would 'turn out to be perhaps the happiest period in their nine years of married life' is a grim one, indeed, and throws into question not only her choice of chapter title but more generally her tendencies towards sentimentality and idealisation (p. 143).

The sad truth is that there simply is not much evidence on which to base an interpretation of Eileen's mind or emotions. This requires Topp to speculate about happenings, motives, feelings and effects. Readers' reception of these speculations will vary depending on their levels of trust in Topp's ability to channel Eileen's spirit. There's nothing that any biographer may have done otherwise – no documentary sources by Eileen's hand left undiscovered – but for this reviewer, the aim of uncovering Eileen O'Shaughnessy from her hiding places in George Orwell's history is here only partly achieved, both as an independent biography and as an extension of the Orwell biographical-critical tradition.

This biography is not a feminist recovery project. Readers will discern this early on from Topp's comment that 'the number of women Orwell relied on and cherished will perhaps be surprising to some, especially those who believe him to have been a bit misogynistic' (p. xiv). A person's dependence on and even passionate attachment to women is not incompatible with their distaste, contempt or hatred for those women or women more generally. To the contrary, the qualities of dependence on the support of the very people we see as lesser, other or subservient is more the norm in human relations than the exception. Eileen, the protagonist of this biography, is valuable as an appendage to George Orwell, someone whose story is measured in the terms indicated by the book's subtitle: *The Making of George Orwell*. There is nothing collected or asserted here that dispels the idea, conveyed by all of George Orwell's biographers, that whether or not Eileen O'Shaughnessy was the making of George Orwell, George Orwell was the unmaking of Eileen O'Shaughnessy. Time and again, lest we'd forgotten the words of Gordon Bowker, Bernard Crick, Peter Davison, Jeffrey

Meyers, Peter Stansky and William Abrahams, Michael Shelden or D. J. Taylor, all of whom provide extensive source material for Topp, Orwell asked Eileen to serve him, to suppress her own ambitions and desires and feelings and finally, to suppress even her own health concerns to advance his ease, obsessions and output. To her credit, Topp becomes more critical of Orwell's sexist behaviours and complacent patriarchal conformity as, chapter by chapter, the evidence of his consumption of Eileen's energy and creativity mounts.

Scholars will admire Topp's recovery of details about Eileen's family of origin and incorporation of reflections of Eileen's female friends Norah Symes Myles, Lettice Cooper and, especially, Lydia Jackson. Norah she had met at Oxford, Lydia at UCL and Lettice at the Ministry of Food. All represent possible answers to the question: 'Who might Eileen O'Shaughnessy have become if she hadn't married George Orwell?' A novelist like Cooper? A writer and translator like Jackson (writing as Elisaveta Fen)? It is more likely she would have finished her coursework in psychology, written a thesis, earned an advanced degree from University College London and built a career in this field. To pursue these perhapses, however, is to indulge in the very kinds of speculative acts that are most intrusive in Topp's biography. What we know is that Eileen was useful to Orwell, that she chose and stuck to a difficult marriage, that she was a good friend, good cook and witty correspondent, and that she left few words, images or effects behind.

BOOK REVIEW

Topp is right to refuse to paint Eileen as a victim, a passive pawn or slave to the machinations of a conniving, genius husband otherwise famous as a standard-bearer of decency and freedom in the West. As Topp demonstrates, Eileen was a spirited, loyal, daring, intelligent, funny, well-educated person, able to understand some if not resist many of the gendered ideologies of her time and place. And here is the real value a more in-depth examination of the histories of Eileen's female contemporaries may have provided the biography. For a similar case, one might have looked to Mamaine (Paget) Koestler, the wife of Orwell's friend Arthur Koestler and identical twin sister of Celia (Paget) Goodman, one of the women to whom Orwell proposed after Eileen's death. Mamaine's letters to Celia, preserved and published by the latter in 1985 as *Living with Koestler: Mamaine Koestler's Letters 1945-1951*, let us see more clearly the vital need for extensive documents if we are to come close to understanding the mind and life of a woman married, and some might argue, sacrificed to literary genius.

If we look next at Inez Holden, Mamaine and Celia's cousin, Orwell's friend and, briefly, lover, and author of seven novels and innumerable shorter works, we see the accomplishments but also the hardships of the single woman's literary life. Finally, and most instructive of all, we can consider Sonia Brownell, Orwell's vivacious, curvaceous second wife who was canny enough to marry him at a point when he (or his estate) could serve her rather than she serve him. It was Mamaine who, in a letter to her twin sister written upon hearing in September 1949 of Sonia's engagement to Orwell, said: 'I think the news about Sonia and George is splendid, and am most impressed by Sonia's courage in making what must have been a very difficult decision. It will of course be wonderful for George, and may save him; in any case I think it can only be good for Sonia to be released from the crushing difficulties of life as a single woman, of finance, or dreary work and solitude' (Goodman 1985: 111).

Reading Eileen's story along with these other women's stories we realise anew how all are unique in their details but similar in their lessons about the effects of sexism on intellectual women's creativity, livelihood and longevity. Was resistance to the sexist conventions of the handmaid's tale that Topp tells possible? Yes. Was resistance profitable? No. Was it comfortable? No. Was it companionable? Not necessarily. But these nos do not relegate the scholar of George Orwell's works to uncritical acceptance of 'St. George' Orwell, the myth of the self-made and self-expressing man of genius described so memorably by John Rodden. And I can't think of a single biographer who does. All confront the difficult history of George Orwell's marriage to Eileen, including the extraordinary abandonments, particularly in the months during her last illness and death alone at the age of 39, in Fernwood House hospital, in Newcastle. The value of Topp's biography as an extension of these previous biographical projects may be determined by readers' reactions to the words 'Poor Orwell' that begin the Epilogue, 'Orwell without Eileen.' Topp will have succeeded if some are inspired to exclaim: 'What about Poor Eileen!'

REFERENCE

Goodman, Celia (ed.) (1985) *Living with Koestler: Mamaine Koestler's Letters 1945-1951*, New York: St. Martin's Press

Kristin Bluemel,
Monmouth University

The Lost Girls: Love and Literature in Wartime London
D. J. Taylor
Pegasus Books, New York and London, 2020, pp 388
ISBN 978 1 64313 315 7 (hbk)

From the author of *Orwell: The Life* (2003) comes this gem of a book, a collective biography of four beautiful young women – Janetta Parladé, Lys Lubbock, Barbara Skelton and Sonia Brownell – whom Cyril Connolly collected and employed at *Horizon*'s offices from its beginnings in 1940 to its last days in 1950. Some of these characters and their associations with Orwell are well known: Sonia as Orwell's widow and literary executor, Connolly as the boy Orwell knew at St. Cyprian's and Eton who went on to become the literary king-maker in wartime London and *Horizon* as the vehicle by which Connolly created those kings. It was in *Horizon* that Orwell first published his miniature masterpieces 'Boys' Weeklies', a large part of 'England Your England', 'Wells, Hitler and the World State', 'The Art of Donald McGill', 'Raffles and Miss Blandish' and 'Politics and the English Language', testament enough of Connolly's taste and *Horizon*'s impact. Taylor's musings on *Horizon*, which he describes in his Orwell biography as combining 'high, if not Olympian, literary aspirations with an indisputable chic' (2003: 276), could very well be the origin of his *Lost Girls* project. Perhaps the contrast between Orwell's big-footed path to the journal's offices in Landsdown Terrace and the elegant circulation of its 'secession of well-bred young secretaries' within sparked Taylor's interest in the glamourous women who helped orchestrate 'Orwell's first introduction to London literary life proper' (ibid: 277).

BOOK REVIEW

Apart from its bearing upon the climate and culture that nurtured Orwell into literary life, *The Lost Girls* is a fascinating exposition of lives and values that, while not exactly lost to scholars, have hovered on the margins of social and literary history. A sign of their relative obscurity is the difficulty of knowing how to find entries for the women in an index. For example, should one search for Brownell, Sonia; Orwell, Sonia; Blair, Sonia; or Pitt-Rivers, Sonia? Taylor throws up his hands in the book proper, identifying the girls by first name. His index covers scholarly bases by guessing at the most common search term (e.g. 'Brownell, Sonia') and redirecting as necessary (e.g. '*see* Orwell, Sonia'). The twisted path one follows through Taylor's index speaks to the central difficulty of these women's lives and our histories of their time: sexism. They did not maintain names of their own, let alone remunerative professions. The girls arrived in the world too rich to be trained for work, too unimportant to be educated, too pretty to be left alone and too idiosyncratic to seek political parties and solidarity. Driven by a constitutional restlessness that made conventional marriage impossible for each, these women adopted art, literature and sexual wandering as a way of life, travelling, in the case of Barbara, all the way to Egypt, where she became the mistress of King Farouk.

Lacking a group identity, the Lost Girls were also generationally lost, too young to be classed with the Bright Young People of the 1920s and too old to be classed with the feminist rebels of the 1960s. Taylor says they provide the bridge between these two generations, showing us how independent, unconventional women born during or right after the First World War and coming of age in the Second could influence an unabashedly, unrepentantly sexist Second World War literary culture. Their distinction as a 'social unit' (p. 17) derives from their quests for autonomy and fulfilment of ambitions without the support of family, feminism, education, professional training or, in some cases, money. The story Taylor tells of their freedoms reads like a novel – a gothic novel at times – luring readers on with delicious quotations from their own and contemporaries' memoirs, novels and letters. Taylor's is a world that appears, in its wartime drudgery, filled with love affairs, sex, high fashion, Ritz dining and bohemian living, with books and art giving lustre to its frame. This book lets us imagine the colours of lipstick and Schiaparelli gowns superimposed on those iconic photographs of grey Blitz living, reproduced in every responsible history or biography of the period. This is not to say that Taylor is irresponsible, but his representations of and attitude towards his protagonists are too delightful to feel there is much duty involved in this required reading.

Both structurally and dramatically, the plump, effete and slightly despicable Connolly functions as the centre of this tale, but Taylor's humorous contempt for Connolly's habits and machinations prevents Connolly from dominating the book the way he dominated the lives of the women who served him and *Horizon*. Taylor's respect and affection for the Lost Girls, evident in his conscientious effort to give their words weight within his narrative, makes them more interesting than the men who talked to them, worked with them, slept with them, married them. There is an incestuous rotation of partners that may make some readers feel slightly woozy, but most will cheer on Taylor's heroines as they survive bombings, abortions, penury and plain old-fashioned unhappiness. Swirling most violently in the maelstrom is the figure of Barbara Skelton, divine of body, demonic of temperament. She makes Sonia seem positively staid by comparison. Orwell had little or nothing to do with Barbara, but his friend Connolly was lucky (or unlucky) enough to sleep with her in the very late '40s while living with one-time fashion plate Lys Lubbock and married to American heiress Jean Bakewell. Connolly was, per usual, playing the women off each other, as he was also and always stringing along the nubile Janetta, hankering after photographer Joan Rayner and keeping tabs on his ex-mistress Diana Witherby. No wonder Orwell felt a failure, with this example before him of the literary man's home life. Neither he nor downtrodden, dutiful Eileen could compete. Of course, once Orwell had really made it as a literary man, he followed in Connolly's path and acquired a *Horizon* girl of his own, though alas he never did get to sleep with her.

Judged among the secretaries at *Horizon*, Sonia stands in a class by herself, admirably in command of most of the day-to-day management of the journal. Today we would regard her as a Managing Editor and give her a respectable salary. Back then, Sonia won praise for competence and efficiency, rebuke for her bossiness and moodiness, but was granted no professional title and certainly no professional pay grade. As late as 2016 her dear friend Janetta took umbrage at the idea of Sonia assuming posthumous credit for anything other than secretarial work, complaining huffily to Taylor: 'Well, she practically tried to make out she was its editor by the end' (p. 337).

Janetta's late-in-life snarkiness about Sonia's editorial pretensions is one example of the kind of interpersonal undercutting that was part and parcel of the Lost Girls' relations with each other. More important, however, is the evidence Taylor provides of their mutual support. Rarely do we get in biographies a sense of conversation between women extending over years, revealing the sororal possibility of London's literary world. *The Lost Girls* is, among other things, a valuable archive of talk between women, preserved in correspondence and memoirs. The inveterate Bloomsbury diarist, Frances Partridge, plays an important role in this regard, documenting over many years the career of her beloved Janetta for whom she functioned as substitute mother and mentor. Through archival sleuthing and adroit citation, Taylor is able to convey diverse patterns of female friendship and relationship, in all their complexity, without measuring the meaning of those relations exclusively in terms of their effects on men. For example, in this book Sonia becomes interesting on her own terms, or on terms Taylor sets up as Lost Girl terms, rather than as a late and rather ignominious appendage to Orwell's story.

The Lost Girls ends with an echo of Orwell's 'Last Man in Europe' with a 'Finale: The Last Lost Girl' set in April 2016 when Taylor made his way to Knightsbridge and the 94-year-old Janetta Wooley Slater Kee Jackson Parladé, a.k.a. the Marquesa de Apezteguia. We find Janetta rich, assured, acerbic, formidable, funny. Taylor records her words about her one-time *Horizon* girlfriends: Lys Lubbock is 'a bit of a nightmare' (p. 336) and Barbara 'a menace' (she was) (p. 337). Connolly, for all his selfishness and lechery, gets off easy: 'He wasn't a bore in any way' (p. 338). This 'Finale' may position Connolly as the planet around which the lost lunar women circle, but it is our ebullient biographer who gets the last stylish word, leaving us in no doubt as to who is in control of this tale. In creating the Lost Girls,

BOOK REVIEW

KRISTIN BLUEMEL

Taylor has recreated the world of *Horizon* and wartime London, giving us a new context in which to read Orwell's life and most important literary productions.

Kristin Bluemel,
Monmouth University

MARTIN TYRRELL

Orwell Reconsidered
Stephen Ingle
Routledge, New York, 2020, pp 156
ISBN 978 0 3673 4479 5 (hbk)

'We would do well not to travel too deeply into the mines of Orwell's journalism without a small sack of canaries' (p. 119), advises Stephen Ingle in this slim, but by no means slight, critical study. Look out, he advises, for Orwell's frequent, and sometimes bizarre assertions: 'At 50, everyone has the face he deserves,' that well-known entry from his final literary notebook, or, my own particular favourite: 'Burglars, as is well known, usually vote Conservative,' which comes from a 1940 review of *The Big Wheel*, by Mark Benney, a former burglar (Orwell 1998a [1940]: 238). Even as an anonymous storyteller Orwell cannot resist the urge to assert. 'All parents are tiresome from a teacher's point of view,' he tells us in *A Clergyman's Daughter*, 'and the parents of children at fourth-rate private schools are utterly impossible' (Orwell 1990 [1935]: 226). Ingle goes on to show how Orwell deploys such sweeping generalisations in serious debate. Responding to Vera Brittain's *Seed of Chaos*, her critique of the Allied air raids on Germany in the last twelve months of the Second World War, Orwell writes: 'No decent person, cares tuppence for the opinion of posterity' – a 'preposterous claim', as Ingle says (Orwell 1968 [1944]: 151; p. 116). As preposterous as Orwell's subsequent assertions from the same polemic – that it is humbug to say that war might be restrained; and no bad thing that others besides young men are being killed; or that calling Germans 'Huns' is worse than bombing them. 'Under which canon of truth telling,' asks Ingle, 'do these gems of wisdom fall?' (p. 116)

Ingle is also rightly cautious of what would today be called Orwell's life writing. The *Wigan Pier* journey, for example. However formative that experience may have been it did not comprise the 'many months' Orwell later claimed in the preface to the Ukrainian edition of *Animal Farm*. It lasted eight weeks in total, one of them spent as a guest of his sister Marjorie and her husband, plus a few days ill in Liverpool and a day or two in Brontë country. Six weeks maximum in the distressed areas, Ingle reckons.

I am less convinced, however, when Ingle turns his scepticism on 'Such, Such Were the Joys', Orwell's bitter account of his time at St Cyprian's preparatory school. How could Orwell have known, Ingle asks, that corporal punishment at the school was administered on the basis of parental income with the result that canings fell disproportionately on the (relatively) less well off. Surely this is Orwell, the socialist author, applying a little class analysis with hindsight? As for the rest – the portrait of the artist as despondent schoolboy ('Failure … behind me, failure ahead of me…' he at one point recalls) – Ingle reminds us that Orwell at St Cyprian's was a high-flyer whose solid academic performance won him a rare scholarship to Eton. Jacintha Buddicom, an early and enduring Orwell crush, remembered him not as a damaged and dysfunctional child, but as a boy precociously ambitious to write and be renowned for it (Orwell 2002 [1952]: 382). To that I would say that children, like adults, know how and when to put on a brave face. Orwell himself writes: 'A child which appears reasonably happy may actually be suffering horrors which it cannot or will not reveal.' Generally, moreover, 'Such, Such Were the Joys' is a reflective essay that comes tempered with an adult sensibility, ending on some mature acknowledgement that a child's perspective on its adult tormentors might, indeed, be exaggeration.

'Every intelligent boy of sixteen,' runs Orwell's knowing narration in *Keep the Aspidistra Flying*, 'is a Socialist. At that age one does not see the hook sticking out of the rather stodgy bait' (Orwell 1956 [1936]: 43). The following year – 1936 – he was a socialist himself. Thereafter, he later claimed in 'Why I Write' (1946), all his serious writing was written to advance democratic socialism. That political purpose, he said, was the making of him as a writer. It was what had lifted his work above empty aestheticism or the humbug of purple prose. Stephen Ingle, however, suggests that socialism was not, after all, the big idea with Orwell and that benchmarked against the likes of George Bernard Shaw, he was not even as especially political writer. 'Orwell,' he comments, 'was only fleetingly active in political life' (p. 108). His membership of the Independent Labour Party (ILP) – a leftist fringe party separate from the Labour Party proper – lasted little more than a year in the late 1930s and 'there was no branch of organised socialism to which he did not show rancour' (p. 111). If 'The Lion and the Unicorn', of 1941, sets out to offer a kind of revolutionary programme, then that programme, Ingle says, 'is as far from concrete as can be imagined' (p. 109).

BOOK REVIEW

MARTIN TYRRELL

Downplaying Orwell's socialism is by far the most radical revision in *Orwell Reconsidered*, and I am not convinced by it. Orwell, once he had become a socialist, never ceased to be one and while I could not say for sure if, as he claims in 'Why I Write', 'every line of serious work' he produced thereafter was written to advance socialism, I think a reasonable case could be made that most of his output was for the cause (Orwell 2001 [1946]: 319). Nor was he rancorous towards the socialists of *all* parties. The Labour Party, of which he became a supporter around 1940, he generally leaves unmolested, its far left especially. He wrote for its paper *Tribune*, greatly admired at least two of its 'big beasts', Cripps and Bevan, and was at pains to quash the idea that *Nineteen Eighty-Four* and Ingsoc were intended as criticism of it. If he had an issue with Labour, it was that it never went far enough for him.

Orwell was not an original socialist thinker – there is no 'Orwellism' – and 'The Lion and the Unicorn' is, indeed, thin on detail, as Ingle suggests. But it is all the same a concise and coherent statement of what its author, and most people at that time, would have understood socialism to mean – that government should control industry and agriculture and thereby the economy as a whole, that it should use this economic power to bring about greater income equality and classlessness, and that it should at least begin the decolonisation process.

There is a clear Marxist side to Orwell's socialism. He was insistent, for example, that socialism was a more efficient economic arrangement than capitalism and that capitalism was evolutionarily 'late' and, therefore, not long for this world. He also claimed, in the years immediately before the war, that fascism and liberal democracy were two faces of the same capitalist coin and, right to the end, he believed that British living standards were artificially high on account of colonialist exploitation. Socialists, he thought, would need to brace themselves for the economic fall-out from decolonisation.

In part, this Marxist influence reflected Marxism's cultural reach at that time, but also the influence of the ILP – an influence that should not, I think, be discounted as readily as it is in *Orwell Reconsidered*. Although, as Ingle says, Orwell was only briefly an actual member of that party, his connection to it dated back to the early 1930s through *Adelphi* magazine and his job at Booklovers' Corner. When Orwell turned to socialism after his *Wigan Pier* journey, it was at an *Adelphi* and an ILP summer school that he learnt his creed. It was through his ILP connections that he went to Spain in 1936, and when he got there, he served in the militia of the POUM (*Partido Obrero de Unificación Marxista* – the Workers' Party of Marxist Unification), the ILP's sister party in the International Revolutionary Marxist Centre.

For the ILP was a Marxist party rather than, as Ingle says, a party that 'included varieties of Marxist and Trotskyite' (p. 110). Its distinctive view of things informs Orwell's final two books of the 1930s – *Homage to Catalonia* and *Coming Up for Air*. It also informs much of his other writing at that time, notably review essays such as his commentary on Clarence Streit's *Union Now*, in which he opposes the coming war with Germany (because he sees Britain and Germany not just as rival capitalist states practising rival forms of capitalism, but as systems of governance – imperialism and Nazism – that he considers morally equivalent).

As Ingle tells us, Orwell's opposition to the war (and his ILP membership) ended sometime in 1939. Ingle dates the change to Hitler's invasion of Poland though Orwell himself put it a little earlier, sometime during the night of 21 August 1939, when he said he had dreamed that the war had already started and that he was supportive of it – 'patriotic at heart' as he wrote in 'My Country Right or Left' (Orwell 1998b [1940]: 271).

BOOK REVIEW

But although Orwell changed his mind about the war, he did not change it about socialism. If anything, the war, at the outset anyway, made him a more enthusiastic socialist than previously. In 'My Country Right or Left' and 'The Lion and the Unicorn' – both written around the time of Dunkirk and the fall of France – he argues that only a revolutionary socialist Britain can prevail against Hitler. Should Britain stay stuck in its old capitalist ways, then the war is as good as lost.

Even when this revolution failed to come about, Orwell remained committed to socialism. Some kind of collective economy was coming, he argued, because capitalism was finished. His main concern was whether the coming arrangement would be totalitarian or democratic. *Animal Farm* and *Nineteen Eighty-Four* reflect his anxiety, deeply felt, that the totalitarian variant might prevail and are attempts at preventing such an outcome.

Ingle, however, says that Orwell was not so much an advocate of socialism as of common decency. In his concluding chapter, especially, he examines common decency both as an aspect of Orwell's worldview and as something of universal value that more than ever needs its advocates. But he offers no succinct statement of what it might be. Going by *Orwell Reconsidered*, decency would appear to apply to justice, equality and truthfulness and, in its British variant, both publicly-funded institutions like the National Health Service and private charitable initiatives such as the food banks set up voluntarily in recent years to try to alleviate poverty. Also, Ingle writes, decency 'encapsulates those values of "Britishness" that ... can be found, for example, in a simplified form in the promises made by every Scout and Guide in Britain' (p. 126). The Scout Promise, care of the Scouts UK website, is certainly concise. It runs:

MARTIN TYRRELL

On my honour
I promise that I will do my best
To do my duty to God and to The Queen
To help other people
And to keep the Scout Law (The Scout Association 2020).

I am assuming that it is the 'help other people' that relates most to common decency and that the Scout Law goes into the detail of that help. The reference to the Queen locates the decency in a particular national context while the reference to God links it to a specific tradition. I think that's a substantial hint that common decency is not a belief system in itself and is, maybe, more a feature of a successful political arrangement than the basis for it: the good behaviour that comes when large numbers of people have co-existed for a reasonable period of time.

Ingle refers in particular to 'The Lion and the Unicorn' as a work in which 'patriotism and democratic socialism come together in common decency' (p. 126). In that essay, Orwell advocates that socialism be established within the existing political set-up. As in the earlier and similarly themed, 'My Country Right or Left', he argues that socialism can be built on the existing structures of the British state and that the patriotism that that state excites, especially in the working class, will empower it.

Ingle also refers to an image Orwell twice used to illustrate the decline of religious faith in Western society. Reviewing Henry Miller's *Tropic of Cancer* for the *New English Weekly* in 1935, Orwell wrote: 'Modern man is rather like a bisected wasp which goes on sucking jam and pretends that the loss of its abdomen does not matter' (Orwell 1968 [1935]: 154). Four years later, in 'Notes on the Way', a two-part essay published in successive issues of *Time and Tide* in spring 1940, he returned to that same image, now couching it in an anecdote (shameful if true) in which he reveals that there was an actual wasp and that he himself was the person that had cut it in half ('a rather cruel trick' is how he puts it). Orwell recalls that only when the wasp attempted to fly 'did he grasp the terrible thing that had happened to him' (Orwell 1998c [1940]: 124). Like that wasp, Orwell writes, we have lost, not our abdomen, but our soul. People can continue, soullessly, for a time, he says, but eventually there is the realisation of what has been removed from them, and of its implications. 'There is no wisdom except in the fear of God; but nobody fears God; therefore there is no wisdom' (Orwell 1998c [1940]: 125). Without the universal fear of divine retribution, Orwell says, we can expect to live in an increasingly brutalising society. It is a powerful and unsettling insight on Orwell's part, one that was to some extent prompted by a reading of Malcolm Muggeridge's *The Thirties*, to Orwell, a 'brilliant and depressing book' (Orwell 1998c [1940]: 124).

How best to react to these new and soulless circumstances? Ingle suggests, rightly I think, that this was a question that greatly exercised Orwell, possibly throughout his writing life. One option he considered was to continue on with religious practice even in the absence of any actual belief. In *A Clergyman's Daughter*, Dorothy, though she loses her faith, goes through the routines of devotion all the same – 'Better to follow in the ancient ways than drift in rootless freedom' (Orwell 1990 [1935]: 249). Orwell, too, went through the motions of religious faith when he was teaching in Middlesex and both his wedding and his funeral were, at his own request, church affairs. Like Dorothy, Ingle writes, Orwell found it impossible to slough off his Anglican 'moral structure' (p. 38).

But going through the motions of faith without any actual faith is surely unsatisfactory. In 'Notes on the Way', Orwell suggests that what is needed in the new, soulless world is 'a society in which men know that they are mortal and are nevertheless willing to act as brothers' (Orwell 1998c [1940]: 125). Such brotherhood, he argues, requires a collective identity. Hence, in his wartime writings he proposed that the basis for that society, and that common identity, should be the British state reimagined as socialist.

BOOK REVIEW

Commenting again on Muggeridge's book, this time in the *New English Weekly* in April 1940, Orwell notes that the author, for all his defeatism and despair, believes in England if in nothing else and has acted on that belief by joining the army, an action Orwell commends. '[A] time comes', he writes, 'when the sand of the desert is sodden red and what have I done for thee, England, my England' (Orwell 1998d [1940]: 151).

In Orwell's writings of the early war years – 'My Country Right or Left' and 'The Lion and the Unicorn' – such patriotism becomes a kind of secular religion that might fill the spiritual void left by the demise of religion proper. The two essays differ. Where 'My Country Right or Left' envisages an actual revolution with red militias and blood on the streets, 'The Lion and the Unicorn' proposes a gentler transformation more in tune with Ingle's common decency. Fittingly for a writer who had previously commended the traditional family unit (his working-class family in *Wigan Pier*, for instance, all at peace, the children contented 'with a pennorth of mint humbugs'), Orwell here imagines the nation itself as a family, one whose principal shortcoming is that the wrong members – 'irresponsible uncles and bedridden aunts' – are at the head of it (Orwell 1958 [1937]: 117; Orwell 1998e [1941]: 401). There is even a suggestion that 'England' might somehow slip imperceptibly from capitalism to socialism without so much as a change of government:

> The Stock Exchange will be pulled down, the horse plough will give way to the tractor, the country houses will be turned

MARTIN TYRRELL

into children's holiday camps, the Eton and Harrow match will be forgotten, but England will still be England, an everlasting animal stretching into the future and the past, and, like all living things, having the power to change out of recognition and yet remain the same (Orwell 1998e [1941]: 409).

It seems fanciful, the more so since the tendency of tradition is ultimately not to revolutionise so much as to conserve. Moreover, tradition is not as gentle as 'The Lion and the Unicorn', with its talk of suet puddings and old maids on bicycles, might suggest. Many have been thwarted, marginalised, and damaged by traditional ideas of gender or sexuality, race and religion. Ingle does not here shy away from the darker side of tradition nor from the unpleasantness of certain of Orwell's own traditional prejudices such as his hostility to homosexuality ('I am not one of your fashionable pansies like Auden and Spender,' he wrote to Nancy Cunard in 1937) or his blanket denunciation of all manner of alternative lifestyles in *The Road to Wigan Pier* (Orwell 1968 [1937]: 67).

Ill-tempered and intolerant comments of that kind surely jar with the idea of common decency. The kindest that can be said of them is that they are of their time and times have changed. Almost all of the things that displeased Orwell, from birth control to breakfast cereals, have become mainstream and commonplace. The nation of red pillar boxes and suet puddings and so forth is no longer the homogeneous family imagined in 'The Lion and the Unicorn.' It is a diverse society and, arguably, a fairly successful one. It is not, I think, the elusive common decency that has enabled this or has held things together during the changes of the post-war decades. Its cohesion is, I believe, down to something Orwell touches on in a further essay on nationhood, *The English People*. Here he refers to the political system of the United Kingdom, which I would agree with Orwell in describing as, at least historically, an *English* system. It is the English parliamentary and party system extended to incorporate Scotland (but not Northern Ireland, which, significantly, has proven the problem part of the Union). Orwell suggests that that system needs to be made to work. 'If the English took the trouble to make their own democracy work,' he writes, 'they would become the political leaders of Western Europe, and probably some other parts of the world as well' (Orwell 1968 [1947]: 31). He does not say, however, what it is about English democracy that is not working and needs to be mended. It is possible that it is the fact that the system is dominated, as he says, by two parties – Conservative and Labour. But to me, that is what has made the system robust and enduring. The common ground between the communities and regions of the United Kingdom is not ethnicity, religion, or culture. It is that they are citizens of the same polity. And it is through the party system that that citizenship has had active meaning, that people who do not know one another, let alone like or respect one another, can yet participate equally in something of consequence – the affairs of the state that governs them. That is the basis for the settled society in which common decency occurs. Ingle is sceptical that it can endure. Orwell might have thought the same.

'During recent years,' Orwell wrote, 'there has been a revival of political activity, but over a longer period interest in politics has been dwindling.' People, he claims, are not voting in 'great numbers' (Orwell 1968 [1947]: 13). It is a complaint that has been often made, and many times, in the years since. And Stephen Ingle, here, also suggests the same: that party politics is ceasing to engage. He writes of 'the total disfunctionality of the current party system of popular representation' (p. 126) in the years since the 2016 Brexit referendum. It is not an unreasonable claim to make but, if it is indeed the case – if the party system of the United Kingdom is broken and dysfunctional – there are some difficult times ahead.

REFERENCES

Orwell, George (1990 [1935]) *The Clergyman's Daughter*, New York: Penguin

Orwell, George (1968 [1935]) Review of *Tropic of Cancer* by Henry Miller, Orwell, Sonia and Angus, Ian (eds) *The Collected Essays, Journalism and Letters, Vol. I*, New York: Harcourt pp 154-156

Orwell, George (1956 [1936]) *Keep the Aspidistra Flying*, New York: Harcourt

The Scout Association 'The Scout Promise' available online at https://members.scouts.org.uk/supportresources/958/the-scout-promise

Orwell, George (1998 [1937]) Letter to Nancy Cunard, Davison, Peter (ed.) *The Complete Works of George Orwell, Vol. XI, Facing Unpleasant Facts*, London: Secker and Warburg p. 67

Orwell, George (1998a [1940]) Reviews of *The Big Wheel* by Mark Benney; *The Lights Go Down*, by Ericka Mann; *The Diary of a Nobody*, by George and Weedon Grossmith, Peter Davison (ed.) *The Complete Works of George Orwell, Vol. XII, A Patriot After* All, London: Secker and Warburg pp 238-240

Orwell, George (1998b [1940]) My Country Left or Right, Peter Davison (ed.) *The Complete Works of George Orwell, Vol. XII, A Patriot After All*, London, Secker and Warburg pp 269-272

Orwell, George (1998c [1940]) Notes on the way, Peter Davison (ed.) *The Complete Works of George Orwell, Vol. XII, A Patriot After* All, London: Secker and Warburg pp 121-127

Orwell, George (1998d [1940] Review of *The Thirties* by Malcolm Muggeridge, Peter Davison (ed.) *The Complete Works of George Orwell, Vol. XII, A Patriot After All:* London: Secker and Warburg pp 149-152

Orwell, George (1998e [1941]) The Lion and the Unicorn, Peter Davison (ed.) *The Complete Works of George Orwell, Vol. XII, A Patriot After* All, London: Secker and Warburg pp 391-434

Orwell, George (1968 [1944]) As I Please, Orwell, Sonia and Angus, Ian (eds) *The Collected Essays, Journalism and Letters, Vol. III*, New York: Harcourt pp 150-153

Orwell, George (2001 [1946]) Why I Write, Peter Davison (ed.) *The Complete Works of George Orwell, Vol. XVIII, Smothered Under Journalism*, London: Secker and Warburg pp 316-321

BOOK REVIEW

MARTIN TYRRELL

Orwell, George (1968 [1947]) As I Please, Sonia Orwell and Ian Angus (eds) *The Collected Essays, Journalism and Letters, Vol IV*, New York: Harcourt pp 1-38

Orwell, George (2002 [1952]) Such, Such Were the Joys, Davison, Peter (ed.) *The Complete Works of George Orwell, Vol. XIX, It Is What I* Think, London: Secker and Warburg pp 356-387

Martin Tyrrell,
Queen's University, Belfast

TIM CROOK

George Orwell, The Secret State and the Making of *Nineteen Eighty Four*

Richard Lance Keeble

Abramis Academic Publishing, Bury St Edmunds, Suffolk, 2020, pp 175

ISBN 978 1 84549 7613 (pbk)

Could George Orwell have had close ties to the spooks? Was the Julia-Winston passionate affair in *Nineteen Eighty Four* the depiction of the classic honey-trap operation in espionage? Was Orwell the quintessential proto-blogger? What kind of a journalist was he? Would he have been the Leveson Inquiry's star witness in the notorious trial of journalism ethics? Would he have been a BBC basher or BBC cheer-leader? What next on the Orwell publishing treadmill after *Orwell's Cough* and *Orwell's Nose*? *Orwell's Throat* or *Orwell's Ear*? Or, as Richard Keeble observes when reviewing John Sutherland's *Orwell's Nose*: 'Sutherland concedes that *Orwell's Bum* 'may be an obliquity too far' (Keeble 2020: 140).

Keeble asks so many questions others have dared not to ask or neglected to even think about asking. He has made a very significant contribution to understanding the life, times and writings of this enigmatic and popular writer. Now Orwell has greater academic focus in universities.

Keeble has pioneered original research and publication about Orwell's importance in the developing theoretical and practical academic discipline of UK journalism. He is also one of the key co-founders of *George Orwell Studies*, and this impressive volume brings together a full range of the many academic papers and articles he has produced on Orwell over the last few years.

He quite rightly explains that in 1999, given the extent of biographical and wide analysis of Orwell's oeuvre, he did wonder whether he had anything original to say. He quickly realised that previous researchers and biographers had neglected to investigate Orwell as a journalist, and then possibly as someone with close ties to the intelligence services. And he particularly appreciated that Orwell's essays and analyses of popular culture predated the French structuralists and post-structuralists, and, indeed, the British Marxists and post-Marxists such as E. P. Thompson and Raymond Williams. Perhaps Orwell actually founded and originated the concept of Cultural Studies…The evidence is identified as multiple commentaries he wrote on apparently trivial subjects such as Donald McGill's naughty seaside postcards and 'crime novels, boys' weeklies, women's magazines, cups of tea, Woolworth's roses, common lodging house, the common toad and handwriting' (ibid: 167).

The book's title, *George Orwell, The Secret State and the Making of Nineteen Eighty Four*, seems to have been coined to compete with some of the other recent *Nineteen Eighty-Four* retrospectives such as Dorian Lynskey's *The Ministry of Truth: A Biography of George Orwell's* 1984 (Picador, 2019) and D. J. Taylor's *On* Nineteen Eighty Four*: A Biography* (Abrams Press, 2019).

I feel Keeble's book has added value in being an informative and entertaining literary, cultural and political scan of Orwell's significance as an author. This is because the essays and articles, split into three sections, forge new perspectives on Orwell's last novel, his journalistic imagination and the afterlife beyond his tragic and untimely death in 1950.

One of the chapters is, in fact, a review of the Lynskey and Taylor books. Throughout the volume, Keeble investigates key Orwellian themes by reviewing new texts that touch on Orwellian matters – a technique and style of literary journalism which Orwell himself turned into an art.

One of the pleasures of this slim volume is that Keeble's crystal pane clarity of style respects the Orwell writing tradition. He avoids the jargon of academic gobbledygook and like the best in journalism tells us so many things that you would not necessarily find in other books about the subject.

There is also a very good argument being run. While the middle section consolidates Keeble's view that Orwell deserves much more recognition as a working journalist, the full transcript of a delightful interview with Orwell's friend and *Observer* editor David Astor discloses that he 'didn't think of him as a journalist. The best things he did for journalism were book reviews. He was a political writer, a literary critic but not a journalist' (ibid: 39-40).

TIM CROOK

He may not have been particularly good at traditional mainstream journalism, but Astor made sure his seminal essay on writing, 'Politics and the English Language', anchored the *Observer* newspaper's style-guide for its journalists.

Could it be that Astor and Orwell, both old-Etonians, shared a disdain for the hacks of Grub Street? Astor had a habit of calling professional journalists 'plumbers' (Lewis 2016). And the more literary and cerebral magazine feature-orientated 'journalists' he would recruit such as George Orwell, Sebastian Haffner and Arthur Koestler were in the higher, more intellectual and cultural realm of periodical 'writers' and 'authors.'

As Keeble says, Orwell thought 'mainstream newspapers were basically propaganda for wealthy proprietors' (Keeble 2020: 121). He was not particularly enamoured of the hack reporters peddling their lies and exaggerated sensationalism.

Keeble succeeds in defining a running theme throughout Orwell's life and writing – the ability to conjure the wry irony of paradox that always had a habit of poignantly hitting home with the sharp edge of truth. At the same time it was often funny.

Orwell has become so much of a lodestone for mainstream journalism. Commentators, reporters and editors continually project so much of their own ideologies, foibles and prejudices on to him. Is it not ironic that there is just one statue iconising journalists outside the BBC's New Broadcasting House in London – that of Orwell himself? He had been on the staff of the BBC for only two years. He did not have anything particularly nice to say about the place. The citadel of broadcasting celebrates a man who left them a legacy of unflattering reflections. His time there had been wasted. He said it had been like working in a mix of an exceptionally badly run girls' boarding school and an asylum.

Yet the quotation adorning the statue on the chain-smoking author of dystopian gloom reminds anyone entering and leaving that '… if liberty means anything at all it means the right to tell people what they do not want to hear'. As Lynskey quite rightly says: 'For Orwell, the truth mattered even, or perhaps *especially*, when it was inconvenient' (Lynskey 2019: 19).

Keeble devotes a lot of his research and writing to speculating that Orwell dabbled in the world's second oldest profession. He says this experience, knowledge and understanding informed the prose, mood and plot of *Nineteen Eighty Four*. There is the close friendship with David Astor who, he says, worked alongside Ian Fleming in Naval Intelligence and in the covert Special Operations Executive during World War II. Astor also employed Kim Philby as the *Observer*'s Middle East correspondent in Beirut until his defection to the Soviet Union in 1963.

There was Orwell's willingness to provide his 'little list' of 'crypto-communists' to the UK's secret Information Research Department (IRD) Cold War propaganda operation. Spooks everywhere had their eyes on Orwell. The NKVD spied on Orwell during the Spanish Civil War and the KGB archives in Moscow kept a file on him. The FBI in Washington D.C. also had a file. And MI5 and Metropolitan Police Special Branch spied on him throughout his life starting when he was 'down and out' in Paris and at the very beginning of his writing career in 1928-1929.

But to what extent was he culturally their all-encompassing double-agent serving the interests of liberty, freedom and human decency? It is amusing to read that Astor rather debunks Keeble's speculation that Orwell may have been a spook: 'I feel certain that he had no link with intelligence' (Keeble 2020: 41). A fair riposte to such an assertion is that an influential intelligence kind of person 'would say that wouldn't they?' However, Astor's biographer Jeremy Lewis is adamant that though he 'admitted to applying to join MI6 shortly before the outbreak of World War Two, I've come across no evidence whatsoever in his archives that he was ever a secret service operative, or that he had any kind of formal relationship with MI6/SIS' (McCrum 2013).

However, Keeble's reading of Orwell's novels, in particular *Nineteen Eighty-Four*, is certainly given credence by D. J. Taylor who confirms that in the relationship between Winston and Julia, Orwell demonstrates 'a fugitive, opportunistic affair between two ill-matched lovers, one of them is very probably an agent provocateur' and that this 'is about the only form of dissension that a totalitarian state allows' (Taylor 2019: 144).

Keeble's critical writing on Orwell maintains a mischievous eye on Orwell's humour. This is exquisitely expressed in my favourite essay in Chapter 8: 'There is Always Room for One More Custard Pie.' Here the contradictory dimensions of Orwell's character are highlighted, namely the two 'f's in Orwell's life – a sense of failure and fun. Only a social democrat with a sense of humour could name his dog Marx. It is also true that a contemporary of Orwell, General Montgomery, had a fox-terrier during the Battle of Normandy he had christened Hitler, which had been a gift from the BBC's War correspondent Frank Gillard.

On matters of waging war, Orwell relished the irony of describing himself being shot through the neck by a sniper while on the Republican frontline in Spain in 1937 and thinking: 'This ought to please my wife … She had always wanted me wounded which would save me from being killed when the great battle came' (Keeble 2020: 76).

Keeble fully understands Orwell's belief that every joke is a tiny revolution and this is so well exemplified when 'Dickens is able to go on being funny because he is in revolt against authority, and authority is always there to be laughed at. There is always room for one more custard pie' (ibid: 81).

And Orwell had a custard pie for Richard Keeble on the occasion he took up the Orwell Society's regular pilgrimage to the barren and isolated cottage of Barnhill on the Scottish Isle of Jura where *Nineteen Eighty-Four* had been written. The investigative and scoop-hunting journalist in Keeble was determined to track down the eldest surviving inhabitant of Jura who could surely reveal the identity of the hitherto unknown fisherman's daughter called Julia whom Orwell may have secretly dated on the island. Could he discover what had 'eluded Davison, Taylor, Meyers, Shelden, Bowker, Crick and Co?' (ibid: 157). Would he find the inspiration for Julia in most probably the 20th century's most influential English-speaking political novel?

After much traditional shoe leather wearing and door-stepping enquiries, including that of the local postman, Professor Keeble was advised to see an 89-year-old lady called Nancy. The village shop advised him that she liked chocolates. After nervously turning up with chocolates, biscuits and a newspaper, he met an elegantly dressed woman who had lived on Jura most of her life and was rather prone to giggling.

This ground-breaking interview proceeded as follows: 'How many times had she seen Orwell? "Several," she says. And that was about all she could say. How did Orwell look: was he tall, brooding, clutching a book? "Ordinary." Oh well: at least I'd spoken to someone on the island who had seen Orwell. But then, on reflection, I am left wondering: had she really?' (ibid: 158).

REFERENCES

Keeble, Richard Lance (2020) *George Orwell, The Secret State And The Making of* Nineteen Eighty-Four, Bury St Edmunds: Abramis

Lewis, Jeremy (2016) David Astor: A king in the golden age of print, *Observer*, 7 February. Available online at https://www.theguardian.com/media/2016/feb/07/david-astor-golden-age-of-observer-journalism-jeremy-lewis

Lynskey, Dorian (2019) *The Ministry of Truth: A Biography of George Orwell's 1984*, London: Picador

McCrum, Robert (2013) Kim Philby, the *Observer* connection and the establishment world of spies, *Observer*, 28 July. Available online at https://www.theguardian.com/world/2013/jul/28/kim-philby-david-astor-observer

Taylor, D. J. (2019) *On* Nineteen Eighty-Four*: A Biography*, New York: Abrams

Tim Crook,
Goldsmiths, University of London

BOOK REVIEW

RADIO REVIEW

Focusing on Five Words: Fascism, Truth, Big, Law and Love

Norman Bissell reviews an innovative series of BBC Radio 4 programmes celebrating the 70th anniversary of the death of George Orwell.

To mark the 70th anniversary of the death of George Orwell, a series of short programmes by documentary-maker Phil Tinline called 'Orwell in Five Words' was broadcast by BBC Radio 4 in January 2020. These words were 'fascism', 'truth', 'big', 'law' and 'love'. It was an innovative approach aimed at seeing what light Orwell could shine on today's problems when, in Tinline's words, authoritarianism is on the march, disinformation, or the fear of it, is everywhere and Orwell's work has never been more urgently relevant. To assist him he enlisted a wide range of academics and writers with specialist knowledge of Orwell as well as those with direct experience of these issues.

The contributors to the first programme on 'fascism' included historians David Dwan and Timothy Snyder and authors Nick Cohen and Dorian Lynskey. The focus was on the changing attitudes of Orwell before and during World War Two. It contrasted Orwell's view that fascism was an advanced form of capitalism, that democracy and fascism were like tweedledum and tweedledee, and his support for the Independent Labour Party's anti-war position with his view in 1942 that objectively the pacifist was pro-Nazi. Political thinker, 'Blue Labour' Lord, Maurice Glasman expressed the view that the word 'populist' was a weak, anaemic term for the far right and advocated Orwell's adoption of patriotism and socialism. Timothy Snyder, a history professor at Yale and author of *On Tyranny*, said that the victors of World War Two were no longer on top of the world, that truth-free communication technology meant that some of the sources of fascism were present today and that some politicians were consciously using the tactics of fascism, the language of violence and divisive 'us and them' rhetoric.

The second programme on 'truth' began with Orwell's 1943 essay Looking Back on the Spanish War in which, as a result of his experience fighting fascism in Spain in 1937, he realised that newspaper reports of the war bore no resemblance to the truth. The media historian and director of the Orwell Foundation, Professor Jean Seaton, said that Orwell understood how propaganda was used to take people away from the bleak harshness of reality, while David Dwan suggested that Orwell's experience working for the BBC during the war made him more aware of how propaganda worked. By 1942, Orwell felt that the very concept of objective truth was fading out of the world. The novelist, Joanna Kavenna, added that Orwell realised that truth was becoming whatever the leader said was the truth. Timothy Snyder argued that totalitarianism replaced truths with myths and that today people were becoming atomised, manipulable and vulnerable to emotional appeals that were not based on fact. In 2016, Russian troll farms were circulating false Orwell quotes and generating fake realities which influenced political decisions in the West. In *Nineteen Eighty-Four*, Winston Smith realises that the resistance is fake and O'Brien tortures him into believing that what the party believes is true *is* true. Orwell was telling us to be sceptical about what is true or false, but not cynical.

The word 'big' is indelibly associated with Orwell's most famous phrase 'Big Brother Is Watching You' and this programme explored the role of big organisations and how they impacted on the lives of individuals. Orwell's distrust of big organisations predated his last novel which was influenced by his experience of an expanding BBC in wartime. His critique of ex-Trotskyist James Burnham's writings on the growth of a new managerial class that could become an oligarchy did not blind him to its relevance to the post-war world. 'Big' was seen as more efficient but led to the individual being subordinated to centralised control. Author Ferdinand Mount made an interesting contribution that revealed that he is the nephew of Anthony and Violet Powell. He said he had read *Animal Farm* at a young age and reported to Orwell that there were no difficult words in it – which pleased him no end. Mount was also head of Margaret Thatcher's Policy Unit in the 1980s which set about giving more powers to individual citizens and emasculating local government. He had shared an office with James Burnham at the New York-based journal *National Review*. Joanna Kavenna stressed how tech giants like Amazon, Facebook and Google were developing alarming new powers. For instance, Facebook had misused big data to alter individual moods back in 2012 and, in the case of Cambridge Analytica, had used psychological profiles of millions of people to influence the results of elections and referenda. However, she was confident that human beings would in the end defeat the unaccountable technocrats.

The 'law' episode began with *Nineteen Eighty-Four* where nothing was illegal because there were no longer any laws. This reflected the reality of lawlessness in Nazi Germany and Stalinist Russia where laws were circumvented by the one-party state. Nowadays, our private lives are subject to surveillance in our homes and through our mobile phones. This led to an interesting discussion about present-day China where Uyghur Muslims in Xinjiang province who had not broken any law were detained in camps because of their alleged potential to commit a crime. A detainee Abduweli Ayup recognised what Orwell wrote about in his last book because of his own experiences. He had been detained for fifteen months and interrogated every day for two months for promoting the Uyghur language. His captors tried to get him to confess to being a separatist and told him 'we are the law'. He was imprisoned and tortured for, in his words, wanting 'to keep my language and culture alive'. The academic Joanne Smith Finley said that the Chinese one-party state was going against its own Constitution in doing this and Muslims were being tortured to confess to imaginary crimes.

The final programme on 'love' continued to make comparisons between *Nineteen Eighty-Four* and the Chinese state today. Joanne Smith Finley spoke about banners outside mosques which were changed to carry the slogan 'Love the Party, Love the Country'. Shades of 'You must love Big Brother'. The Chinese government's 'people's war on terror' has led to widespread surveillance, saturation policing and hundreds of thousands of detentions. These actions were reminiscent of Orwell's view of the Moscow Show Trials in 1938 when Old Bolsheviks confessed to false conspiracies because they had been brainwashed. American psychologist Robert Jay Lifton suggested that the Chinese had learnt about these methods of extracting confessions when they were in Moscow and had contributed the idea of re-education to their 'thought reforms'. This was taken further by Mao Zedung's programme of rote learning, 'correct thoughts' and self-criticism. Uyghur Muslims are being forced by torture to renounce their religion and their culture. As in *Nineteen Eighty-Four*, the family is being targeted with representatives of the state coming into people's homes. Now in exile, Mihrigul Tursun spoke movingly of being afraid to tell her parents what had happened to her. Uyghur family members are being made to learn to love their oppressor, but they continue to resist.

What emerged from the five programmes is that we still live in a world shaped by the politics of the mid-twentieth century and that Orwell's profound political insights still retain their ability to cut through the obfuscations of the seemingly all-powerful. I was disappointed that there was not more emphasis in the series on President Trump's and Prime Minister Johnson's application of Steve Bannon's playbook and Russia's involvement in seeking to break up the European Union which threaten the future of Western democracies. Bannon's racist brand of populism denounces liberal elites and 'fake news', stokes fears of immigration and loss of identity, spreads lies and is being employed by far right politicians in Italy, Hungary, France and elsewhere. It would be good if more Orwell programmes of this calibre could be made, although the current Conservative government onslaught on Britain's public broadcaster makes this unlikely. The series is well worth listening to and is available until January 2021 on BBC Sounds at https://www.bbc.co.uk/programmes/m000dk0z.

NOTE ON THE CONTRIBUTOR

Norman Bissell is the author of *Barnhill: A Novel* (2019) about George Orwell's last years and the poetry collection *Slate, Sea and Sky, a Journey from Glasgow to the Isle of Luing* (2008), both published by Luath Press. A former principal teacher of history and area officer of the Educational Institute of Scotland, he is the Director of the Scottish Centre for Geopoetics and is a member of the Writers Guild GB Scottish Committee. www.normanbissell.com.

RADIO REVIEW

REVIEW ESSAY

Throwing Light on Orwell's Crucial Quarrel with Comfort

Richard Lance Keeble

One of the delights of Orwell scholarship is the way in which it constantly throws new light on events and characters marginalised or ignored in the conventional biographies. Take Alex Comfort, for instance. He tends to receive only a passing mention following his intriguing poetic skirmish with Orwell in the columns of *Tribune* during the Second World War. After Comfort (later to gain international fame following the publication of his *The Joy of Sex*) promotes his anarchist pacifist response to the war against the Nazis in a fifteen-stanza poem, 'Letter to an American Visitor', Orwell responds with an equally vitriolic Byronic satire 'As One Non-Combatant to Another (A Letter to Obadiah Hornbooke)' (see Crick 1980: 438-439, 443; Bowker 2003: 291-292, 299, 304; Meyers 2000: 218, 219). He does not appear at all in Robert Colls's biography (2013) nor in Michael Shelden's (1991).

Eric Laursen's excellent text, *The Duty to Stand Aside: Nineteen Eighty-Four and the Wartime Quarrel of George Orwell and Alex Comfort* (AK Press, Chico, California and Edinburgh, 2018) examines the Comfort/Orwell relationship in forensic detail and, in the process, explores a number of crucially important issues relating to pacifism, anarchism, war-fighting, freedom of expression, the value of friendship – and the cancer of secrecy.

ORWELL – FROM ANTI-WAR TO PRO-WAR

Between returning from the Spanish civil war in 1937 to the outbreak of the Second World War in 1939, Orwell adopted an outspoken anti-war position. Any war would, he maintains, do nothing more than extend imperialist possessions and interests. Laursen notes Orwell publishing an article in *New Statesman and Nation*, in 1937, advocating 'anti-war agitation' on these grounds:

1. That war against a foreign country only happens when the moneyed classes think they are going to profit from it.

2. That every war when it comes, or before it comes, is represented not as a war but as an act of self-defence against a homicidal maniac ('militarist' Germany in 1914, 'Fascist' Germany next year or the year after). The essential job is to get people to recognise war propaganda when they see it, especially when it is disguised as peace propaganda (Laursen 2018: 23).

In 1938, Orwell joins the anti-war Independent Labour Party (founded in 1893 as a left-wing organisation to further the interests of the working class and by the 1930s a left alternative to the Labour Party) and in September signs the ILP manifesto 'If War Comes We Shall Resist It'. Early in the following year, he contributes a book review to *Peace News*, the journal of the pacifist Peace Pledge Union, and in March, with German troops marching into Czechoslovakia, Orwell writes to his friend, the anarchist poet Herbert Read, arguing that war preparations will lead to 'some kind of Austro-Fascism' in Britain (ibid: 23-24). But then Orwell's views suddenly change. As he recounts in 'My Country Right or Left' (1940), during the night before the announcement of the Russo-German pact in August 1939, he dreams the war has begun and it becomes clear that he is both relieved and that, as a patriot, he will support the war effort (Taylor 2003: 272).

SETTING THE BROAD POLITICAL CONTEXT

One of the many strengths of Laursen's text is the way in which it places the Orwell/Comfort spat within a broad historical and political context. Here, he indicates the strength of the anti-war movement during the lead-up to war: up to 175,000 Britons were members of pacifist groups in 1940. But then many like Orwell suddenly shifted their allegiances – including philosopher C. E. M. Joad, Labour MP Philip Noel-Baker and Storm Jameson, novelist and president of English PEN (Laursen op cit: 24). Following the evacuation from Dunkirk and the appointment of Winston Churchill as Prime Minister, Britain begins to execute a policy of 'area' bombing 'in which the RAF deliberately targeted large areas, whole cities, for indiscriminate attacks' (ibid: 27). As Laursen comments: 'No other nation had ever adopted such an approach, not even the Axis powers in Spain; the Luftwaffe's attacks on Britain never reached the same intensity' (ibid). In May 1942, the RAF Bomber Command launches its first – unsuccessful – attempt to wipe out a whole city, Cologne. Operation Gomorrah in August against Hamburg kills up to 40,000 people 'almost as many as the entire German Blitz over England – although the final death toll will probably never be known' (ibid: 28). In total, some 600,000 European civilians are killed and more than a million seriously injured as a result of British and American air raids, with 7.5 millions left homeless. During the conflict, the War Cabinet will even contemplate area attacks using mustard gas on civilians. When reports emerged in 1943 that the

REVIEW ESSAY

RICHARD LANCE KEEBLE

Nazis may be planning to use biological weapons, the US begins to produce such weapons as well. Moreover, the tight blockade imposed on the Nazi-occupied continent by the British navy leads to famine in Greece while food shortages kill thousands of Jews confined to ghettos in Warsaw and other cities.

Yet Laursen is always careful to 'balance' his reporting. Here he records the Luftwaffe dropping more than 57,000 tons of high-explosive incendiary bombs on British cities killing over 43,000 civilians and leaving up to 139,000 injured. According to the RAF, the bombing campaign was not gratuitous but a matter of desperate necessity while the naval blockade, it could be argued, helped reduce the duration of the war – perhaps by years (ibid: 34-35).

ORWELL'S CHANGING RESPONSE TO THE BRITISH WAR EFFORT

By 1941, Orwell is already confiding to his diary concerns over the lack of self-criticism among the patriotic clergy. 'God is asked "to turn the hearts of our enemies, and to help us to forgive them, to give them repentance for their misdoings and a readiness to make amends". Nothing about our enemies forgiving us' (ibid: 35). Later, he writes in his diary: 'The authorities in Canada have now chained up a number of German prisoners equal to the number of British prisoners chained up in Germany. What the devil are we coming to?' (ibid: 40). And in an unpublished letter to *The Times,* he argues that this sort of response only shows how Britain is prepared to 'descend to the level of our enemies'.

ORWELL REVIEWS COMFORT FOR THE FIRST TIME

It is only now that Orwell comes into contact with Alex Comfort – reviewing his first novel, *No Such Liberty*, for *Adelphi*, the journal edited by Orwell's friend Sir Richard Rees which has published some of Orwell's earliest essays and which has recently taken up a pacifist position. As Laursen indicates, Comfort was an only child of lower middle class parents, only able to send him to Highgate School, then to Cambridge and his medical training 'with the help of scholarships and a good deal of scrimping and saving' (ibid: 22). By the 1940s he becomes part of the New Romantics group of young poets – including Nicholas Moore, John Bayliss, George Barker and Henry Treece – who oppose the 'insanity' of a political system that instigates the mass slaughter of war (ibid: 20). *No Such Liberty* is the story of a young pathologist and his wife who flee Nazi Germany only to face persecution in Britain. In his review, Orwell says it's a 'good novel as novels go at the moment' but is essentially a tract pushing the message of pacifism. In any case, he argues, the pacifist is objectively pro-Nazi.

He follows this up with a letter in the March/April 1942 issue of *Partisan Review*, in which he attacks 'quisling intellectuals' including Comfort ('a "pure" pacifist of the other-cheek school'). Comfort responds in the September/October issue challenging Orwell's insinuation that pacifists would make peace with a German occupation. Rather, pacifists would be 'the only people likely to hold genuinely anti-fascist values'. And so the controversy between the two men continues. Orwell now acknowledges that Comfort has written a poem he values greatly ('The Atoll of the Mind') but rejects totally his argument in a recent letter to *Horizon* that 'adversity tends to produce great literature'. Laursen sums up the two positions astutely:

> Orwell hoped, at least faintly, that the government-directed wartime economy would become a stepping-stone to socialism, the overthrow of the class system, and the marginalization of the Right. … Comfort and the other anarcho-pacifists were far more cynical. Who were the people directing the war effort? they asked. What were their aims and why should people on the left suddenly trust them? (ibid: 51).

Laursen goes on to criticise Orwell's position: 'Other than occasionally voicing vague hopes for a libertarian-socialist revolution, he seems never to have thought through the implications of allowing Churchill and his companions to lead the nation in its fight against the very regimes many of them had tolerated before the war' (ibid: 51).

VITRIOL IN VERSE

Following the *Partisan Review* exchanges, Comfort and Orwell send respectful letters to each other. Orwell explains some references he had made to 'Jew-baiting of a mild kind' in an *Adelphi* article while Comfort compliments Orwell on his essay 'The Art of Donald McGill' and even thanks him for the negative review of his novel. Then, on 4 June 1943, *Tribune* publishes Comfort's 15-stanza poem 'Letter to an American Visitor' in which he mocks Churchill's stirring speeches as 'the dim productions of his bulldog brain', condemns the Church's willingness to preach that 'bombs are Christian when the English drop them' and even suggests – in a direct jibe at Orwell's BBC arts programmes – that the country's literary giants are willing to turn out propaganda in exchange for avoiding military service (ibid: 60). Two weeks later, on 18 June, Orwell responds with his own Byronic satire 'As One Non-Combatant to Another (A Letter to "Obadiah Hornbrooke")'. Laursen suggests that at the heart of the poem 'is an almost anguished attempt to justify his own decision to offer his services and his reputation to a government he knew was trafficking in lies and propaganda, and to distinguish himself from the professional liars' (ibid: 63). He writes:

RICHARD LANCE KEEBLE

> It doesn't need the eye of a detective
> To look down Portland Place and spot the whores
> But there are men (I grant, not the most heeded)
> With twice your gifts and courage three times yours
> Who do that dirty work because it's needed;
> Not blindly, but for reasons they can balance,
> They wear their seats out and lay waste their talents.

Orwell, ever ready to surprise, moves ever closer to Comfort after this intriguing poetic tiff. In a letter he praises Comfort's poetic gifts and says he is reconsidering his views on literature and the war. Laursen comments:

> It was easier, perhaps, for Orwell's thoughts to turn in this direction in the summer of 1943 when the German army was being driven, agonizingly, from Russia and the Allied invasion of occupied Europe was in the planning stage. ... Additionally, Orwell was clearly tired of defending his decision to work for the government. Two months later, he resigned from the BBC 'after wasting 2 years in it' (ibid: 65).

On becoming literary editor of *Tribune*, Orwell invites Comfort to contribute articles. So the following June, he contributes – mischievously – a poem titled 'The Little Apocalypse of Obadiah Hornbrook' in which he again satirises wartime propagandists. The poem draws furious letters from readers. In response, Orwell reassures them that he does not agree with poet's sentiments but stresses the journal's open policy towards contributors – though they would never print an article in favour of anti-semitism, for instance. He even takes on some of Comfort's argument: 'I should be the last to claim that we are morally superior to our enemies and there is quite a strong case for saying that British imperialism is actually worse than Nazism' (ibid: 69).

The strength of Laursen's book is that it unearths the fascinating story of Orwell's ongoing debates with Comfort – largely ignored in previous biographies – which reveal the depth, complexity and ever-changing nature of Orwell's positions on war-fighting and pacifism. After Comfort, in January 1944, issues a manifesto to subscribers of *Poetry Folios* protesting at the ways in which modern warfare relegates the principles of international law 'in favour of the unreserved pursuit of total warfare', the pacifist campaigner Vera Brittain publishes *Seed of Chaos: What Mass Bombing Really Means* comprising eye-witness accounts of the saturation bombing of German cities. In his 19 May 1944 'As I Please' column in *Tribune*, Orwell responds to Brittain and suddenly shifts away from his neo-Comfortian line, backing – appallingly – the strategy of indiscriminate bombing. All talk of limiting and humanising warfare is sheer humbug, he says. And in a column two months later he argues ('bizarrely', according to Laursen) that it is 'probably somewhat better to kill a cross-section of the population than to kill only young men...' (ibid: 80).

OUTRAGE OVER ATTACK ON FREEDOM PRESS

In November 1944, Special Branch raids the premises of the anarchist Freedom Press in response to a manifesto published in *War Commentary* calling on members of the armed forces to practise mass disobedience once the war is over, if not before. Immediately, a Freedom Press Defence Committee is formed with Orwell as vice-chair (the only office he ever accepts), Herbert Read, chair, and George Woodcock as secretary. Laursen comments perceptively: 'The Freedom Press raid must have had an especially powerful effect on Orwell, given his experience of political persecution in Spain' (ibid: 85). In an August 1944 'As I Please', he writes:

> War damages the fabric of civilisation, not by the destruction it causes ... not even by the slaughter of human beings but by stimulating hatred and dishonesty. ... By hating [your enemy], by inventing lies about him and bringing children up to believe them, by clamouring for unjust peace terms which make further wars inevitable, you are striking not at one perishable generation but at humanity itself (ibid).

Orwell moves increasingly closer to his anarchist/pacifist colleagues. The two writers he attacked in his 1942 *Partisan Review* column, Woodcock and Julian Symons become close friends, in January 1946 he accepts an invitation to address the London Anarchist Group on 'Trends in Russia's Foreign Policy', and he allows the anarchists Vernon Richards and his wife Marie Louise Berneri to take photographs of him at his home relaxing with his son, Richard. Laursen comments: 'This is not as paradoxical as it might seem. Whatever Orwell's objections to anarchism, anarchists themselves were an important component of the anti-communist left with which he generally identified himself, starting in Spain, and he couldn't help but notice their viewpoints overlapped with his' (ibid: 86).

Orwell next joins his pacifist/anarchist colleagues in condemning the nuclear bombing of Hiroshima and Nagasaki in August 1945. Writing in *War Commentary*, Comfort says bluntly that 'the men who did this are criminal lunatics'. For his part, Orwell, in *Tribune*, argues that the discovery of the atomic bomb would intensify trends apparent over the last dozen years with a few superpowers dominating the world. 'The Bomb, because of the industrial resources needed to produce it, would reinforce and speed up this grim trend which foreshadowed the dystopia he was already turning into compelling fiction in his manuscript of *Nineteen Eighty-Four*' (ibid: 89-90).

RICHARD LANCE KEEBLE

In a comprehensive account of the launch of the book at the Golden Notebook bookstore in Woodstock, New York, Carol Biederstadt reports Laursen as suggesting that 'Orwell won the battle' with Comfort for it 'was clearly necessary to oppose Hitler'.[1] Believing there exists a 'need to take the activist role that Comfort envisaged', however, he believed Comfort had ultimately won their 'ideological war'. Biederstadt continues:

> He elaborates on this in the final pages of *The Duty to Stand Aside*, where he draws attention to the fact that whether or not current governments label a military action a 'war', modern assaults continue to sacrifice civilians. He cites, for example, Associated Press statistics that claim there were between 9,000 and 11,000 civilian casualties in the 2017 'assault against Islamic State forces in Mosul, Iraq'. But neither the Iraqi government, the US-led coalition, nor the Islamic State itself would acknowledge the numbers, even though most of them came from Mosul's morgue. ... If Comfort were alive, these revelations would have shocked but not surprised him, registering as yet another example of the irresponsibility of the State, carrying us one step further in the decline of sociability and another step toward barbarism. His answer would doubtless be the same one he offered during World War II and the nuclear build-up of the post-war decades: Be responsible. Disobey (ibid: 151-52).

DYSTOPIA AND AFTER

Laursen criticises Orwell's dystopian masterpiece for saying little about how the elites of the three superstates come into being other than through the simple lust for power. He suggests that Comfort offers a 'partial answer' in his treatise which appears shortly after Orwell's death in January 1950 titled *Authority and Delinquency: A Criminological Approach to the Problem of Power*. His strategy for ending the regime of delinquents in authority has six elements: education, experiments in communal living; increasing workers' control of production; 'propaganda' and 'instruction' of both children and adults to make sociability a more prominent part of character formation; psychiatry to help the individual to reject and resist 'bad institutions' – plus public resistance and the willingness to disobey. Overall, Laursen is in sympathy with these views. 'Comfort's proposals were rooted in a belief, shared by others on the left, not only that human nature could be improved, but that such improvement was now necessary to keep the human race from destroying itself' (ibid: 105).

Comfort's later fame with the publication of *The Joy of Sex* in 1972 is mentioned but Laursen strangely fails to take this as a cue to explore the ideas about sexuality and sex repression which play such an important role in *Nineteen Eighty-Four* – particularly in the descriptions of the secret, passionate affair between Winston Smith and Julia. In *Barbarism and Sexual Freedom* (1948), Comfort argues that coercion or institutions sponsored by the state and other such religious or civil bodies have no place in sexuality – and any necessary revolution in the individual's sexuality will equally require a revolution in the social order (Marshall 2008 [1992]: 596).

ORWELL'S 'LITTLE LIST'

Having developed this friendship with Comfort his final act is, astonishingly, to betray him. In May 1949, Orwell sends a list of names of crypto-communists to his friend, the glamorous Celia Kirwan, who has taken a job at the government's recently set-up secret propaganda unit, the Information Research Department. One of these – alongside Charlie Chaplin, historians E. H. Carr and Isaac Deutscher, J. B. Priestley, Paul Robeson, Orson Welles, Upton Sinclair – is Alex Comfort. On his potential to collaborate with the communists, he writes: 'Potential only.' Worse is to come: 'Is pacifist-anarchist. Main emphasis anti-British. Subjectively pro-German during the war, appears temperamentally pro-totalitarian. Not morally courageous. Has crippled hand. Very talented' (ibid: 105). Laursen is rightly highly critical of Orwell's action. While his coverage is again deliberately 'balanced' giving the 'understanding' reactions of Christopher Hitchens and Timothy Garton Ash, he ends with these strong words:

> Though Orwell's submission to the IRD was not a blacklist – he wasn't seeking to get anyone fired from their job – it brought Comfort and dozens of other individuals to the attention of a state intelligence apparatus that might abuse that information. And while many of these individuals were already strongly identified as leftists, being tagged as unreliable by another prominent writer of the left could only have put them at greater risk, given the atmosphere of the time (ibid: 121-122).

FINAL REFLECTIONS

One of the many strengths of Laursen's book is to highlight Comfort's anarcho/pacifist views – views which are so rarely considered in the mainstream media – nor even in the academy. Yet there are long and highly significant traditions of both anarchism and pacifism. As Peter Marshall stresses in his 818-page, comprehensive history of anarchism: 'Although often associated with violence, historically anarchism has been far less violent than other political creeds. ... Moreover, a tradition which encompasses such thoughtful and peaceable men as Godwin, Proudhon, Kropotkin and Tolstoy can hardly be dismissed as inherently terroristic and nihilistic' (Marshall 2008 [1992]: ix). Mohandas Gandhi, the leader of Indian Independence, was a kind of pacifist anarchist, always opposed to the centralised state and the violence it engendered. He was particularly inspired by the writings of Leo Tolstoy, Henry David Thoreau's essay on *Civil Disobedience* (1849) and John Ruskin's

RICHARD LANCE KEEBLE

Unto This Last (1860). Carissa Honeywell, for her part, places Comfort within a modern tradition of pacifist theory and practice which embraces the work of Herbert Read, Paul Goodman, Colin Ward and Murray Bookchin (Honeywell 2014). Given more space, Laursen would probably have sought to situate the Comfort/Orwell spat in this broader historical context.

The study is also useful for highlighting the ways in which Orwell's thoughts shifted, often dramatically, over time. One moment he is fervently opposed to the approaching war with the Nazis; then suddenly following a dream he switches to an equally firm commitment to supporting the war effort. And this allegiance shifts down many contrasting lanes – he even supports indiscriminate bombing. But then, after the raid on the anarchist Freedom Press, he shakes off a habit of a lifetime and actually joins a committee set up to defend it. Orwell was, after all, a journalist and author determined to bash out as many words as possible in his short life. Not surprisingly, given the pressures, his views shifted as his moods changed.

The spat with Comfort also highlights the dark side of Orwell's complex, contradictory personality. There is no excusing those nasty few words he wrote about Comfort in his secret list to British intelligence. It is all the more shocking given the friendship which appears to have developed between the two men. Orwell was certainly no saint. But then he never claimed to be one. And no wonder he asked for no biography to be written. He had a lot of secrets which he clearly wanted the world never to know.

NOTE

[1] https://orwellsociety.com/the-comfort-of-pacifism/, accessed on 22 June 2020

REFERENCES

Honeywell, Carissa (2014) Bridging the gaps: Twentieth-century Anglo-American anarchist thought, Kinna, R. (ed.) *The Bloomsbury Companion to Anarchism*, London: Bloomsbury pp 111-139

Marshall, Peter (2008 [1992]) *Dreaming the Impossible: A History of Anarchism*, London: Harper Perennial

Richard Lance Keeble is Professor of Journalism at the University of Lincoln and an Honorary Professor at Liverpool Hope University

George Orwell Studies

Subscription information
Each volume contains two issues, published half-yearly.

Annual Subscription (including postage)

Personal Subscription

UK	£30
Europe	£33
RoW	£35

Institutional Subscription

UK	£100
Europe	£115
RoW	£120

Single Issue copies (subject to availability)

UK	£15
Europe	£17
RoW	£20

Enquiries regarding subscriptions and orders should be sent to:

Journals Fulfilment Department
Abramis Academic
ASK House
Northgate Avenue
Bury St Edmunds
Suffolk, IP32 6BB
UK

Tel: +44(0)1284 700321
Email: info@abramis.co.uk